Brown Paper Press
Long Beach, California

RELAX, IT'S JUST GOD

HOW AND WHY TO TALK TO YOUR KIDS ABOUT RELIGION WHEN YOU'RE NOT RELIGIOUS

Wendy Thomas Russell

Brown Paper Press
6475 E. Pacific Coast Highway, #329
Long Beach, CA 90803

FIRST EDITION

Designed by Andrew Byrom

Library of Congress Control Number: 2014955707

ISBN 978-1-941932-00-1
ISBN: 978-1-941932-01-8 (ebook)

14 13 12 11 10 / 10 9 8 7 6 5 4 3 2 1

For my husband, who is my heart,
and my daughter, who is my heaven

ACKNOWLEDGMENTS

I'd like to thank my parents, James and Nancy Thomas, whose love and encouragement led me to where I am today. And Jennifer Thomas Gravois—my sister, friend, confidante, and editor; she is the first lucky thing that ever happened to me.

I wouldn't have written this book without the early and enthusiastic support of my dear friends Pernilla Göst, Jenny Marder Fadoul, Jennifer Volland, Tim Grobaty, Catherine Gritchen, Veronica Jauriqui, Kim Mishra, Peter Thompson, Valerie Takahama, Erin Einarsson, Lucy Watson, and Heather Wood Rudúlph. Very special thanks for a variety of reasons, go to Dale McGowan, Will Shuck, John Pope, Chris Bartley, Larry Thomas, Gene Russell, and Carol Russell.

But most of all, I'd like to thank my husband, Charlie, and daughter, Maxine. All the best ideas in this book came from them, one way or another.

TABLE OF CONTENTS

Part Two: A New Direction

Part Three: Dealing With Sticky Issues

INTRODUCTION

Talking openly with children about sensitive subjects is hard. It always has been. In my parents' generation, the three-letter taboo was S-E-X. My sister was thirteen when my dad gave her "The Talk." It was the eighties, and my dad dodged it the way any educated man of his time might have. He tossed her a sex-education book and said, "Read this, but don't do it."

Luckily, things have changed. Discussing sex isn't scary now—or quite so scary anyway. Americans are more open with their children than ever before. Modern fathers don't flinch when their daughters ask about that thing dangling between daddy's legs after a shower. Many parents have no more trouble talking with their kids about sex than teaching them how to spell it.

But progressive thinking has a way of replacing certain taboos with others. And today, for a great many parents, there is a new three-letter word: G-O-D.

My daughter, Maxine, was barely five years old when she piped up from the backseat on the way home from preschool one day.

"Mommy," she said, "you know what? God made us!"

I felt like a cartoon character being hit in the back of the head with a frying pan. My heart raced. I'm quite sure I began to sputter. Visions of Darwin and the evolving ape-man raced through my mind, followed closely by my childhood image of the big guy upstairs in his flowing white robes. I couldn't speak. And, in the awkward silence that followed, I was forced to confront the truth: The idea of talking to my kid about God—and, more specifically, about religion—scared the bejesus out of me.

I swallowed hard and forced myself to speak.

"Well," I said, "Who is God?"

Now, I don't remember if Maxine actually said "duh," or whether she simply bounced a "duh" look off the rearview mirror. But I can tell you that the "duh" message came across loud and clear.

"He's the one who made us," she said, her eyebrows knitted.

"Okay... well, what is God doing now?" I tried for casual.

Again with the nonverbal "duh."

"God is busy making people and babies," she answered.

This information could not have been delivered to me with more certainty. My little girl, who had never heard an utterance of the word "God" in our house, aside from decidedly ungodly uses of the word, now had it all figured out thanks to a Jewish classmate who also happened to be her very first boyfriend. I was beaten to the punch by a cute preschool boy.

I let the subject drop, but my chest constricted all the way home. It stayed that way for hours. Why hadn't I been prepared for this? What was I supposed to say now that she was getting her information from this boy at school? What words should I use? Was I to sit her down and tell her that evolution, not God, was responsible for her existence? Was I to impose my own beliefs on her, the way other parents seemed to be doing? Or should I leave her alone to explore on her own timetable? What was the difference between guidance and pressure anyway? What was I willing to "let" her believe, and what wasn't I? As a science-minded non-believer with a generally non-confrontational personality, I was stumped by how to handle the situation.

Luckily for me, I have a husband who is cool under pressure. Later that day, after I'd rather breathlessly presented him with all the facts of the *disastrous* car ride, I asked him, "What if she believes in God?" His answer, my wakeup call, has become a mantra I repeat often. He said, "It's not what Maxine *believes*, but what she *does* in life that matters."

What I took from this was: *Relax . . . it's just God.*

So I set aside my own irrational concerns and began to talk with my kid about God—lots of gods, actually.

And it was good.

Still, each time we hit a new channel of thought, I would sometimes feel that familiar tightening in my chest. It happened when she started talking to her religious friends about her own doubts about God. It happened when a fellow kindergartener told her that people who don't believe in God go to "a very bad school."

In those early days, a lot of things caused me anxiety because, in those early days, there was a lot I just didn't know. I turned to books and websites, but no single source offered the answers I was seeking. I began interviewing parents, then parenting experts, then secular leaders, researchers, authors, psychologists, and religious scholars. In August 2011, I started a blog for secular parents, and the following year I circulated an online survey to non-religious parents all over the United States.

My work has connected me to thousands of non-religious—and progressively religious—parents, all going through similar experiences. Some are atheist or agnostic. Others consider themselves humanists, searchers, or New Age spiritualists. Still others are religious, but non-traditionally so; that is, they loosely associate with a religion but want to teach their children about lots of belief systems, give their kids a choice when it comes to theology, and raise kids who judge people on the content of their character, not the fundamentals of their faith.

Neither religious conservatives nor anti-religious zealots, these parents occupy a broad middle ground. They do not wish to push children into one single system of belief, but rather to raise kids who are both open-minded and well-informed.

Like so many other parenting authors, I wrote the book I wanted to read. It is full of information and advice from experts, fellow parents, and me. Lots and lots from me. But none of it is gospel. Skepticism and independent thought are to be valued and exercised at all times. It's true that many of the concepts raised in these pages are unique to non-religious parents, but most apply to open-minded religious parents, too. Just as most religious believers pick and choose the beliefs that make sense to them, so should you pick and choose from this book what makes sense to you.

I haven't always done everything right. I have stumbled sloppily through more than a few conversations along my own journey and regretted my word choices now and again. But, because the conversations keep coming, I've almost always had a chance to right my wrongs, to clarify my position, to bring a new perspective to each situation. The point here is not to be perfect—as my daughter says, "That would be boring"—but to give us something to aim for.

And forgive me if I cite Christianity more than other religions. It is not out of bias either for or against Christianity but because that is the religion most American children are likely to encounter early in their lives.

Among other things, this book will show you how to:

• speak confidently, openly, and truthfully with young children about your beliefs, or lack thereof, in a way that promotes kindness, compassion and critical thinking.

• successfully navigate family strife and interact peacefully with religious relatives.

• teach children to be accepting and supportive of others' religious beliefs without tolerating the intolerance of others.

• talk about death without the familiar solace of religious imagery.

• introduce religious literacy into your household without burdening you or boring your child.

• help kids better understand and appreciate religious peers, while coping with and vaccinating against the sting of insensitive or harmful remarks.

Non-religious parents are by no means a cohesive unit, and our struggles are hardly singular. But most of us—whether we be atheist, agnostic, humanist, deist or nothing at all—share a common goal: To raise wise, open-minded, and happy kids who can choose their own religious (or non-religious) identities for themselves. What many of us lack, however, is a clear path for how to get there.

Over the last four years, I have distilled what I've learned from research, interviews, and personal experience into a concrete approach to talking to kids about religion when you're not religious. I hope you will join me on this adventure. I hope you will tell your friends. Because exposing kids to various brands of spirituality and religion (not to mention non-religious philosophies) is not only fascinating and surprisingly fun; it also has the potential to make the world a better place.

Like the "sex talk," discussions about God may come up sooner (and differently) than you had pictured. It's your obligation to embrace it. After all, if you're not prepared to explore ideas of God, religion, and faith with your curious child, someone else will do it for you.

Someone cute.

PART ONE *O We of Little Faith*

CHAPTER ONE *Who We Are*

In the spring of 2013, while reporting on the effects of a devastating tornado in the tiny town of Moore, Oklahoma, CNN newscaster Wolf Blitzer stood amidst heaps of debris and interviewed residents about the town's loss of life and property. Moore is one of the thousands of pin dots along America's Bible Belt, and Blitzer was all too aware of that when interviewing Rebecca Vitsmun, a mother whose family had opted to flee their Moore home rather than try to wait out the storm. The Vitsmuns' decision to flee had been a good one; their home was among hundreds left in ruin.

Dwarfed by wreckage on one side and broadcasting equipment on the other, a smiling Vitsmun bounced her nineteen-month-old son in her arms and talked with Blitzer about how lucky she felt to have escaped tragedy. Their home was gone, but they were not.

"You're blessed," Blitzer told Vitsmun warmly. "I guess you gotta thank the Lord, right? Do you thank the Lord for that split-second decision?"

There was a slight hesitation, then Vitsmun laughed awkwardly.

"I'm actually an atheist," she said.

Until relatively recently, it might have been reasonable for a news reporter to assume that a Bible Belt mother was a Christian. Historically, non-believers have been relegated to the sidelines and spoken of in whispers when spoken of at all. You might be an atheist or agnostic, but—like homosexuals not long ago—you wouldn't dream of talking openly about it.

But a new paradigm is at work.

We Americans are abandoning these religious answers at record speed. Today, sixty million people in the United States are unaffiliated with any religion.[1] That's a full 20 percent of the population—up from 8 percent in 1990 and 2 percent in the late 1950s.

As a result, disbelief has gone public. Atheist and humanist groups have cropped up all over the country. Washington recently got its first non-religious lobby, the Secular Coalition of America, and President Barack Obama made political history when he included the faithless in his 2008 inaugural address. "We are a nation of Christians and Muslims,

Jews and Hindus, and non-believers," Obama told a roaring crowd. At a mass at the Vatican in 2013, then-newly elected Pope Francis spoke of spreading a "culture of encounter" where Catholics would judge people not on their beliefs, but on their good deeds.

"The Lord has redeemed all of us, all of us, with the blood of Christ: all of us, not just Catholics. Everyone! 'Father, the atheists?' Even the atheists. Everyone!" Pope Francis told his followers. "We must meet one another doing good. 'But I don't believe, Father, I am an atheist!' But do good. We will meet one another there."[2]

Skeptics have found countless support groups online, and religious lampooning that would have been widely considered blasphemous not long ago makes up some of the Web's most popular memes. (One shining example is the Church of the Flying Spaghetti Monster, a mock religion invented in reaction to the Kansas State Board of Education's decision to permit teaching intelligent design in 2005.)

Add to this the popularity of "New Atheist" activist/authors Richard Dawkins, Sam Harris, and the late Christopher Hitchens, as well as the countless celebrities who publicly tout their disdain for organized faith, and we begin to see that America's irreligious are a force to be reckoned with.

Author David Niose pointed out in his 2012 book, *Nonbeliever Nation: The Rise of Secular Americans*, that an unprecedented era is underway. Routinely marginalized for too long, secular Americans have "begun to stand together as a unit and demand recognition, respect and equality."[3]

Amen, right?

Well, sort of.

While secularism is clearly on the rise, this country is, by no means, secular. It's true that most Christian denominations have diminished, but Christianity is still a major force in America. Mormon churches continue to gain members nationwide, and non-denominational mega-churches are rising up in nearly every state. About 70 percent of the overall population self-identify as Protestant or Catholic, and 34 percent describe themselves as "born again" or "evangelical" Christians.[4]

Many faithless Americans—including some of those in high-profile positions in government and business—hide their lack of religion from others out of fear of reprisal. Out of 533 members of the 113th U.S. Congress, for instance, only one person described herself as religiously unaffiliated.[5] Although this may speak to a lack of diversity among elected officials, it seems far more probable that some officials are politically motivated to affiliate with a religion.

Still, with each passing year, huge strides are made. There is no doubt that, taken as a whole, we of little faith have finally found our voices. And we aren't afraid to use them.

The Rise of the Nones

Barry A. Kosmin is the founding director of the Institute for the Study of Secularism in Society and Culture and a professor at Trinity College in Connecticut. He's also the author of the American Religious Identification Survey (ARIS), which is conducted every ten years and aims to track the religious leanings of the American public.

"There's a kind of ebb and flow to this," Kosmin told me in an interview, his voice still heavily influenced by his native Britain. The United States always has "gone through great awakenings and secular revivals."

But nothing, Kosmin said, had prepared him for the striking shift evident in the results of the 2001 ARIS. Not only had the 1990s—a decade of relative peace and prosperity in America—dealt losses to all of the big-hitters in Christianity (Catholics, Baptists, and mainline Christians), but a catchall category marked "other" had skyrocketed—from 14 million to 29 million.[6] The leap was unprecedented. For the first time in history, Kosmin said, these "others" represented the fastest growing religious group in America. In fact, he recalled thinking, the "others" weren't "others" anymore at all. The "others" were going to need their own category.

Kosmin's team of researchers set to work considering better labels, including *non-religious*, *non-faith*, and *non-affiliated*. But the researchers rejected all of those. The "non" part bothered them.

Non-affiliated would be like calling people *non-white*, Kosmin said. "We didn't want to suggest that 'affiliated' was the norm and everyone else was an 'other.' Nomenclature is quite important in these things."

Lacking anything better, Kosmin began referring to this unnamed group as the "Nones", a shortened version of "none of the above." He didn't expect it to stick.

"It began as a joke," he said, "but now, like many of these things, it has taken on its own life."

But why? Why has organized religion been hemorrhaging members while the Nones continue to rise? The answer to that lies in a multitude of converging realities—including the country's economic stability.

As Kosmin observed, religious convictions fluctuate on a societal level in direct relation to a perceived need for external comfort. It's the reason "comfortable" people tend to be less religious than those whose lives are in chaos. Kosmin cited affluent Japan, where some 84 percent of the population claims no personal religion, versus impoverished Haiti, where the figure is 1 percent.

"The more your life is helpless," he said, "the more you look for external assistance."

But the economy is not the only factor in religion's losses.

Phil Zuckerman is one of the country's foremost authorities on atheism in the United States. He opened America's first secular studies program at California's Pitzer College—a program devoted to the study of non-religious people, groups, thought, and cultural expressions. Zuckerman told me that people walk away from religion for anthropological, psychological, and sociological reasons. Advances in science, globalization, and exposure to people of different faiths (vis-à-vis the Internet) have begun to outweigh stagnant religious dogma.

Niose touched on this in *Nonbeliever Nation:* The Internet is making people more open because it's creating access to other points of view. And at the same time, communities are arising. Thomas Paine once said that his mind was his church. Now, for many their churches exist on the Internet. American independent streaks are another part of the shift, Zuckerman said. Many are tired of the sanctimonious dictates, forced morality, and herd mentality that often accompany Western religions. He said there is a growing distrust in religious institutions—caused, for example, by clergy abuse scandals. And there is a backlash against the Religious Right and its steadfast opposition to gay rights, women's rights, reproductive freedom, secularism in schools, scientific progress, environmentalism, and even the separation of Church and State—a concept embedded in the First Amendment of the United States Constitution.[7]

Particularly when it comes to young people, Zuckerman said, religion's role in vitriolic politics, world conflict, and domestic acts of terror also have been major turn-offs.

"Younger generations' tolerance for the endless disputes of religion," he said, "is waning fast."

What's In a Name?

I would be remiss if I didn't mention that, when it comes to religion, labels are becoming increasingly problematic. Yes, labels convey information, instill a sense of belonging, and help organize the disenfranchised, but they also are used to pigeonhole individuals, prejudge them, stereotype them, and put them down. As a result, many people shy away from them altogether. Even the *Nones*—a rather unthreatening term—has weathered its fair share of opposition, especially from those on the more spiritual end of the non-religious spectrum. The term is too dismissive, they argue. It sounds too much like *nothing*, and their response is, "I'm not nothing."

Others complain that it's a term empty of any real meaning at a time when America could really use some more nuanced language to describe people's beliefs. Consider a recent Pew Research Center study, which revealed that a relatively high percentage of those "unaffiliated" with religion (i.e. Nones) engage in traditionally religious behavior.[8] For example:

• **Thirty percent** of the religiously unaffiliated report that they are "absolutely certain" of the existence of a God or universal spirit, and 27 percent attend worship services on a yearly, monthly, or even weekly basis. Many unaffiliated Americans give to faith-based charities, celebrate religious holidays, and accept religion as an important part of their culture and ancestry.

• **Three-quarters** of all those unaffiliated with religion believe that religious institutions do a great amount of good for society—bringing people together, strengthening community bonds, and playing an important role in helping the poor and needy. And half believe that religion "protects and strengthens morality."

On the other hand, 8 percent of those affiliated with religion report that religion is of little or no importance in their lives, and 20 percent say they are not certain about the existence of a higher power. Perhaps most surprisingly, a full 15 percent of those affiliated with religion consider themselves spiritual but not religious.

As a writer, I have grappled repeatedly with how best to reach my intended audience; should I use *secular, non-religious, unaffiliated, non-traditional, progressive*? I've settled on *non-religious* or *secular* in most cases, but even those can be misleading. Does a *non-religious parent* refer to only an individual who does not have a religion, or does it refer to anyone who has chosen to raise children outside the restraints of one specific religious doctrine? The difference may seem academic, but these slight variations make huge differences to people like Kosmin, who are trying to assess people's beliefs, and to people like me, who are trying to get their books in front of the people who might benefit from them.

So what is a None exactly? The following is a list of the most common labels that fall in Kosmin's catchall category. (There are many others.) You'll notice that most of the terms are not mutually exclusive.

Apatheists	Those who are indifferent to belief/disbelief or consider the subject meaningless.
Agnostics	Those who believe that the existence of God is unknown and unknowable.
Atheists (Positive)	Those who assert that no god exists.
Atheists (Negative)	Those who lack a belief in any god.
Brights	Those who belong to a socio-cultural movement promoting a "naturalistic" world-view—based in nature with no supernatural forces.
Deists	Those who believe in the existence of a god as creator of the universe but reject all organized religion and supernatural events.
Freethinkers	Those who form opinions about religion on the basis of reason—rather than tradition, authority, or established belief.
Humanists/ Secular Humanists	Those who embrace ethics, compassion, social justice and naturalism and attach primary importance to human matters, rather than the divine or supernatural.
Naturalists	Those who believe the universe is devoid of general purpose and indifferent to human needs or desires.
Pantheists	Those who reject the idea of a "person-god" but believe that the "holy" manifests itself in all that exists.
Pluralists	Those who accept all religious paths as equally valid.
Rationalists	Those who hold that reason and logic are the only true sources of knowledge.
Skeptics	Those who believe that continuously and vigorously applying methods of science is the only way to arrive at explanations for natural phenomena.

Searchers	Those who belong to no belief system or world view but are still open to ideas and actively searching for the truth.
Spiritualists	Those who are spiritual—which is an undefined term but generally refers to people who are open to the sacred but more interested in personal well-being and development.

Of all these labels, one is by far the most problematic, and that is, of course, *atheist*. In so many circles around this country, and throughout the world, *atheist* is used as an epithet—a synonym for *arrogant* at best and *evil* at worst. Also, atheism increasingly (and unfairly) connotes anti-religious or anti-God sentiments.

Atheists are still one of the most disliked groups in the United States, currently banned by the Boy Scouts and less likely than any other religious group to be elected president.[9] And atheists continue to be misread and misunderstood. Any doubt about that was laid to rest, for me at least, in October 2013, when Oprah Winfrey all but denied the atheism of Olympic swimmer Diana Nyad during Winfrey's weekly talk show "Super Soul Sunday."

Nyad called herself an atheist, but went on to explain that she could "stand by the beach's edge with the most devout Christian, Jew, Buddhist . . . and weep with the beauty of this universe and be moved by all humanity."

Oprah's response? "Well, I don't call you an atheist then. I think if you believe in the awe and wonder and the mystery, then that is what God is."

The implication was that disbelief is somehow a failure to see the magnificence of life and nature, when, for most atheists, nothing could be further from the truth.

If Oprah's got atheism wrong, it's no wonder so many people with atheistic views prefer to stay away from the label itself. Famed astrophysicist and *Cosmos* host, Neil deGrasse Tyson, is a great example.

"I am often asked, in an accusatory way, are you atheist?" deGrasse has said. "The only thing I am is a scientist. I don't associate with a movement. I'm not an ism. I think for myself."

DeGrasse's understandable hesitancy to adopt a non-religious label is only part of what makes American religiosity so difficult to track these days. Another is that people adopt labels that don't really describe their true belief systems. A person may be culturally Catholic or Jewish or Hindu but hold no supernatural beliefs whatsoever.

"We make a distinction between belief, belonging, and behavior,"

Kosmin said. "People can believe without belonging, belong without believing, and they behave in different ways."

Nothing in this business, he said, is black and white—and there are a thousand shades of gray.

The only way to grasp a person's true faith?

"Put them on the couch," he said, "and ask them."

First, I Lost Hell

When I was a kid, growing up in Northwest Missouri, my town had one grocery store, two banks, and more than a dozen Christian churches. Religious diversity was limited to various brands of Protestantism. Even Catholics were hard to come by. In those days, there was no pressure to include multiple faiths in community holiday celebrations because there were no other faiths in the community. The mere idea of living a life without Jesus Christ was considered weird in the extreme.

And so, like all the kids I knew, I considered myself a Christian—but it was mostly a cultural thing in my family. My mom spoke of God in the vaguest of terms. I never saw my Dad worship anyone besides William Shakespeare, Huckleberry Finn, and Louis Armstrong.

Still, devout wins out in small towns, and, growing up, I spent a lot of hours in churches, looking at the cross and contemplating how that image fit into my life.

I wasn't committed to the Passion of the Christ necessarily, but I definitely bought into the mainstream Christian narrative: God is in heaven, hell is for sinners, and Christianity is the only reasonable choice in the marketplace of world religions.

Even those beliefs began to unravel after high school when I moved away from home and headed to college. Almost immediately, I began to question the whole hell thing. I couldn't fathom that nice people would suffer eternally simply for being born into other religions, or for being ignorant, or for having a skeptical mind. Any God that would do that wasn't a benevolent God. And the God I knew was, if nothing else, good.

So I lost hell, which also meant I lost Satan. And once Satan was out of the way—well, the dominos kept falling. Within the year, I was calling myself *agnostic*, and then *atheist-leaning agnostic.*

"If I had to jump off on one side of the fence," I once told a friend, "it would be the atheist side."

That was 1992.

In the decade that followed, I didn't think much more about my views on faith. For a long time, I adopted a "Don't Ask, Don't Tell" policy. I didn't ask people about their beliefs, nor did I offer up my own. I married a man who shared my worldview, and, beyond that, religion just didn't matter to me. I felt no need to make it a topic of conversation.

That worked out great for about thirteen years. Then something changed.

I had a kid.

CHAPTER TWO *What We're Doing Wrong*

For thousands of years, much of human experience has turned on a handful of questions: How did the world come to be? What will happen to us when we die? Why are we here? How should we behave? Why do bad things happen?

These questions are the basic building blocks of philosophy, religion, physics, sociology, anthropology, and dozens of other fields of study. And, yet, they are so simple that even a child could ask them.

And most children do.

When you were a child, your parents may have passed on the answers they received from their own parents—a brew of culture and custom, environment and experience, perception, and fear. For most, the answers were some variation on: God created the world, runs the afterlife, and wrote the rules. Case closed.

But for millions of Americans, those answers no longer suffice. Secular parents, particularly first-generation secular parents, often find themselves squeezed between the limited—sometimes painful—views they grew up with and their new views, which may not lend themselves so simply to talks with kids.

Jennifer Newton is a thirty-four-year-old California native. Raised in a Christian household, she was repeatedly assured that faith was a necessity and that turning away from religion would result in dire consequences. More specifically, she was told that non-believers burn for eternity in a lake of fire.

Newton has left all those beliefs behind. She knows morality exists independent of belief in a higher power, and now considers hell a myth. She still harbors resentment about some of the things she witnessed in her Christian high school—the expulsion of a gay classmate, for instance, and the lifelong harm the expulsion caused that classmate. Now that she's a mother, she is determined to give her daughter something she never had growing up: a choice.

Sometimes, though, Newton feels paralyzed by her own upbringing. She lacks role models and a community of like-minded non-believers. And emotional issues, such as dealing with her fundamentalist-Christian mom, await her like quicksand. She wants to think she's prepared, but she fears she isn't.

"It's like the Wild West," she told me. "I have no reference for this."

As any mom or dad can attest, parenthood in general is a journey into another world. Often suddenly and for the first time, we realize the capacity of our hearts, the complexity of our desires, and the extent of our limitations. Before kids, we might have thought we had it all figured out; after kids, we know better.

When Maxine was born, I was relieved to learn that a lot of parenting seemed to come naturally to me. It was as though I had this arsenal of skills buried deep within me that I had never known existed. Change a diaper? Check. Distinguish between a tired cry and a hungry cry? Not a problem. Keep my baby entertained? That's what ceiling fans are for.

I got this, I found myself thinking pretty darn often.

But then, as time passed, and Maxine began to move and talk on her own, I began to notice the, well, weaker areas in my parenting arsenal. There were problems I couldn't easily solve, questions I couldn't easily answer—either because I never received the answers myself during my childhood or because the answers I received in childhood didn't work for me anymore.

God was a biggie.

Walking a Tightrope

Non-religious and spiritually progressive parents are no different than any other parent; it's our challenges that are different—different from devoutly religious parents, yes, but also different from each other. How each of us approaches religious discussions, both philosophically and practically, depends largely on our own experiences, background, and values.

As such, the challenges we face when it comes to addressing theological issues with our kids vary widely. Parents who live in religiously conservative communities may worry about indoctrination from others. Those who resent religion may struggle to keep their own attitudes from clouding their children's views. Parents with positive, or even neutral, experiences may face guilt about raising children without religion. Those who were taught morals through religious references may be uncertain about how to instill morality in their kids without them.

In 2012, in an effort to zero in on the most common day-to-day challenges for non-religious parents, I circulated an Internet survey to non-religious parents throughout the United States.

Although wholly non-scientific, the survey was answered by more than one thousand people from all fifty states (plus Guam and several countries outside the United States), none of them from the same household. They came from cities and suburbs, large towns, small towns, and rural areas. Most were mothers with children under the age of twelve; about 25 percent were fathers. A full 72 percent of the parents said they had been raised in religious homes—almost all of them Christian—but had left their faith behind.

I asked all the parents about their backgrounds and their philosophies on life, about how they were raising their children, and what, if any, difficulties they'd encountered in discussing religion with their children.

These were the top ten challenges cited in the survey.

1. Indoctrination: Not knowing how to be honest without indoctrinating kids into one way of thinking.

2. Language: Fear of saying something to their children that would be repeated in mixed company.

3. Family: Having to contradict religious family members while trying to keep peace in the family.

4. Age-Appropriateness: Not knowing what's age-appropriate for children to hear.

5. Resentment: Keeping their own negative experiences or resentment out of conversations with their children.

6. Death: Facing conversations about death without the comforts of heaven or an afterlife.

7. Tolerance: Separating the idea of religious tolerance from the idea of tolerating religious hatred or abuse.

8. Confusion: Fear of confusing a child.

9. Belief: Fear that if a child hears about religion, she or he might start believing it.

10. Religious Literacy: Limited knowledge of religion or religious stories.

Most parents said they walked a bit of a tightrope when it came to navigating religion with their kids. Many talked about how tricky it was to teach children reason, logic, and the value of skepticism, while also allowing them to see the world through their own eyes.

Many found it challenging to strike a healthy balance between pride in their own views and respect for those of others, between encouraging a close relationship with Grandma without encouraging wholesale acceptance of Grandma's beliefs.

A New Hampshire mother of five told me, for instance, that her biggest problem was "having to firmly contradict what my children hear from one or two of their religious playmates, without telling my children what to believe, and all the while maintaining a positive tone toward the other children and hopefully creating an atmosphere of acceptance and openness in my home."

What's more, these parents weren't always sure how to be honest about religion, and their own experiences with it. Some struggled with insecurities and doubts and felt ill-equipped to take questions. Others worried that they would confuse or disappoint their kids, or say the wrong thing, or send mixed messages.

"It's challenging to express my own beliefs," one Virginia mother said, "while conveying that my child should respect that many others have different opinions."

In some religious communities (and you may be in one) raising children without spirituality is judged as immoral, selfish, even cruel. Some parents told me they felt pressured by relatives to take their kids to worship services; to take part in rites of passage that were meaningless to them personally; to give their kids the structure of faith, regardless of their own doubts.

Often, non-believing parents found it hard to be true to themselves without setting their kids up to be ostracized by their peers or stealing their children's freedom of choice.

"I am very concerned that even having a neutral outlook toward religion will result in my children being bullied for not being Christians," a mother told me. "I also do not want them to learn to lie or not stand up for themselves. I'm torn about this dilemma. I have time to work it out because they're very young, but I am upset by the idea of their having to endure persecution for being in a chosen minority."

Our Most Common Follies

Researcher Christel J. Manning is college professor, a mother, and a non-believer. While teaching courses at Sacred Heart University in Connecticut between 2005 and 2007, she traveled throughout the United States to interview secular couples—about 60 in all. What resulted was the country's first academic study into non-religious parenting, whose results have since been published in the journal *Sociology of Religion.*[10]

Manning found several distinct worldviews held by religiously unaffiliated parents and identified five strategies parents employ when incorporating religion in the lives of their children. Some parents, she said, went right back to embracing the religion of their youths, presumably for the sake of the children. Others joined alternative religious organizations—such as the Unitarian Universalist Church, which touts spiritual guidance in a community setting without the dogma of traditional belief systems.

A third group engaged in what Manning called "outsourcing." They enrolled their children in, say, Hebrew School or Catholic catechism classes—while remaining non-religious at home—all in the hopes that the children would learn what they needed to know from there.

A fourth group took it upon themselves to provide religious instruction at home, although, she noted, most of these parents felt they had been unsuccessful at doing so.

But by far the most common approach, she said, was the fifth: absolute silence. When it comes to religion, Manning told me, a large number of parents "completely ignore it."

There is a sixth approach, as well, one that Manning didn't touch upon on in her study. Some parents, mostly militant atheists, indoctrinate their kids against religion by teaching them, to the exclusion of most other messages, that religion is not a valid worldview and should not be taken seriously.

Here we take a quick look at three of the most problematic of these approaches, and what makes them so problematic.

1. Returning to religion for the 'sake of the kids.'

For some, religion is just too compelling to release completely. Some parents believe the benefits children can glean from religious participation outweigh their own personal beliefs. They may even see their own "truth" as confusing matters. For these reasons, and others, many non-religious parents feel they have no choice but to return to a religious life for the sake of their children.

To be clear, I am not talking about parents who simply expose their children to a particular religious culture through classes or worship services, but then talk openly at home about all religions and belief systems and the importance of choice. I'm talking about parents who keep their own doubts private and instead become fully engaged in religion—attending weekly religious services, urging their children to become members of a religious organization, allowing their children to believe that prayer is a necessity and hell is a reality. The whole shebang.

Phil Zuckerman, the sociologist at Pitzer College, said religion is, indeed, a difficult thing for many first-generation secular parents to shed completely. Whether or not a person's memories of religion are positive or negative, they come to symbolize for parents how things "ought to be." Parents may go through the motions, Zuckerman said, because the motions are familiar. "Definitely," he said, "people tend to recreate what they know."[11]

Surprisingly, this happens even when those memories aren't positive.

"Parents may think: 'I hated going to Hebrew School, but I had to do it and my kid's going to do it, too,'" Zuckerman said. "Parents may not care as much if their kids reject it, but may say, 'At least I'm giving them something to reject.' It takes such a strong ideological position to say, 'No, that was bad, and I'm not going to put them through that.'"

Of course, not all secular parents have negative experiences with religion. Manning herself told me that she was raised on what she calls "a healthy dose of religion" and still looks back on the sermons, prayers, holidays, rituals, symbols, costumes, food, and family with fondness and warmth. Years later, even after she'd left her faith behind, those traditions stuck with her. It's what made her feel so conflicted when it came time to talk with her own daughter about religion.

"Even though I left it behind," she explained, "religion was a positive thing for me as a child. I have really fond memories."

Some parents believe their children *need* spiritual guidance; that it's unfair to leave them without the possibility of God to share their hard times with or heaven to look forward to. Oftentimes, Manning said, this guilt is exacerbated by the belief that religious children do better than non-religious children. For instance, she said that some studies over the years have suggested that teens who regularly attend religious services experience lower rates of depression, sexual promiscuity, and drug use than children raised in secular households.

"It's pretty compelling," Manning said of these studies. "The only problem, of course, is that if you look at it very carefully, it seems like the benefit that youth get from religion is being a part of a community—a community of caring adults that offer them activities that are meaningful."

In other words: It's not about the faith at all.

The main problem with returning to religion for the kids is also the most obvious: Parents are indoctrinating their children into a belief system that doesn't make sense to them personally. As Manning said, there is no integrity in it. Parents are essentially lying to their kids.

And what's so moral about that?

2. Indoctrinating kids against religion.

We don't often hear the word *indoctrination* in relation to secularism, but it does exist. Whether by accident or intention, some atheists choose to present their own point of view to the exclusion, and detriment, of most others. And just like religious indoctrination, anti-religious indoctrination can breed prejudice and bigotry.

But, first, a definition. Indoctrination can mean many things—from "formal teaching," on the one hand, to "coercively causing people to act or think on the basis of ideology," on the other. As a practical matter, it may help to think of indoctrination as a sort of halfway mark between simple suggestion and full-on brainwashing. It doesn't require threats or abuse, but it does require a strong influence over someone—sort of like parental guidance on steroids. For the purposes of this book, you can be reasonably sure you're indoctrinating your kids if you teach them the following:

- **Your way is the only right way to believe.** In this context, *right* means *good*; it does not necessarily mean *true*. This is because most people assume that what they believe is true—and there's nothing wrong with that. But truth doesn't always equate with benevolence or decency. In other words, it's okay to think other people's beliefs are wrong; it's another to assume they're bad.

- **People who disagree with these beliefs are less moral, less intelligent, and less worthy of respect.** This concept moves past personal belief to actively disparaging people who see the world a different way, thus suggesting to children that those who believe differently are "lesser than" in a universal sense.

You can see right off the bat how religious people run the risk of indoctrinating their kids by suggesting that religion is synonymous with morality. But anti-religious people run the risk of indoctrination, as well, particularly when they suggest to children that people who believe in the supernatural lack intelligence or reason. In both cases, pretty strong judgment calls are being made, and neither of them are very nice—or true.

There is no way to tell how many anti-religious parents are intentionally indoctrinating their kids. Some 90 percent of the parents I surveyed said they opposed indoctrination of any sort.

But it *is* happening. Let's make no mistake about that.

Jim Morrison is among an elite group of teachers in the United States who have been hired to teach World Religion to public high school students. He has been teaching in Red Wing, Minnesota, for nearly twenty years, and the students love him. Not only does he insist on teaching religion from a historical standpoint, he has no qualms with criticizing religion—even the popular ones. Morrison frequently asks his students questions like, "Did God create man or did man create God?" He introduces his students to different models of reality, including atheism and agnosticism. He treats all religious figures equally.

As you can imagine, he has been the subject of protest from the Christian Right in his community. He said he has been accused of "injecting my own ideas into the course, misinterpreting the Bible, and generally being offensive to Christians."

Once, during a Red Wing town hall meeting on the subject of his class, a local pastor yelled out: "Why can't you just tell the students what other religions believe? Why do you have to make them think?" Even some ministers in the audience had to laugh at that one.

But religious fanaticism is only part of what makes Morrison's job challenging. The anti-religious fanaticism, he told me, is equally problematic.

"I have had countless students enter my class with an attitude of hostility toward religion," he said. "Consequently, rather than truly trying to understand religion as a social phenomenon and how religion plays a role in diversity and culture, they have been raised by their non-believing parents to simply dismiss it outright. As a parent and teacher I want my kids to be non-judgmental. I want them to be skeptical thinkers. And I want them to understand religion, not condemn religion."

"It is my personal opinion," he added, "that children need to be raised to be 'good question-raisers' and not 'quick answer-givers.'"

3. Giving religion the silent treatment.

By far, the road most traveled in the world of secular parenting is also the quietest.

"In our household, religion just doesn't exist," said one of my survey respondents, a Wisconsin mother of five. "It's not something I think about or discuss in relation to our lives."

"There is no need to discuss it," another parent told me. "We know that there are religions, but like other people's underwear, it's none of our business. It's not that interesting."

Manning found this to be the view of most of her study subjects, as well.

"They were too busy with other things to give much thought to how to deal with religion in the lives of their children," she said.

On the surface, it may seem that avoiding religion is not a bad strategy. Parents are not put in a position to lie or to verbalize things they may not have figured out for themselves. They may sidestep conflicts with religious family members. And many parents reason that saying nothing is better than indoctrination; by allowing kids to figure out religion for themselves, parents guarantee that they don't push their own views on their kids. Plus, avoidance lessens the chance that their children will be ostracized by religious peers, does it not?

"I would discuss it more," one mother told me, "but I don't want [my children] to become targets at school. Our community is terribly religious."

A Wisconsin mother of three had this to say: "In Wisconsin people are generally churchgoers but they are also private enough not to ask others about religion. By avoiding the subject we haven't had any problems, although my husband tells the children to say they are Lutheran if anybody asks."

See how avoidance can become a stepping stone to flat-out lying? Funny, that.

Turning our backs on religious conversations carries a laundry list of unintended consequences, none of them pleasant. Kids uninformed about religious matters have no frame of reference when they hear the term "Garden of Eden" or see a Star of David hanging in a car window or groups of people putting fresh fruit before a Buddhist shrine. They may be confused about why their friends seem to have been given a set of facts that they haven't. Some children end up feeling self-conscious, left out, even embarrassed by their lack of knowledge. They don't understand why Jesus died on a cross, why Muslims pray on the ground, or why a thing isn't kosher. And when religion is avoided, there's no chance to talk about religious tolerance.

Christine Tsien Silvers, a doctor and mother of three small children, grew up in a non-religious household in Montana. Her mother's family was Jewish and her father's was Christian, but Silvers was exposed to neither. She was among a number of people I've interviewed who have been raised within the cone of religious silence and wish they hadn't been.

"My mother said to tell, if anyone asked, that we belonged to the 'interdenominational church,' which I couldn't pronounce—so never had a chance to say."

Silvers believed for years that Easter was simply a time to go on egg hunts and celebrate bunnies. "I didn't know until college—at the Massachusetts Institute of Technology, no less—that Easter was a religious holiday at all."

Elizabeth Claire, a retired mother and grandmother from Virginia, had a similar experience. When she was twelve, her sick grandmother—whom she'd only seen a handful of times—called her to the bedside and asked Elizabeth to "always read the Bible."

"I had no idea what a Bible was or where to get one—until years later, my sister's boyfriend swiped a Gideon's Bible [from a hotel] and gave it to me as a gift," Claire said.

She read it when she was eighteen, and it astounded her. *Adam and Eve, The Coat of Many Colors, Daniel and the Lion's Den.* She knew all these stories by heart—having found them among the other children's books at school. But she'd had no clue they'd come from "the book that Christians believe is the word of God."

Lauren Covello works in a publishing house outside Philadelphia. Her father wasn't just non-religious; he was openly anti-religious. Instead of talking with his children about different beliefs, he dismissed all of it as brainwashing. As a result, Covello told me, she never had a chance to understand religion—what attracts people to it, what makes it so meaningful.

"My parents claimed we could be anything we wanted to be," Covello recalled, "but they never exposed us to religion, and I'm pretty sure they would have laughed if I said I wanted to be a Buddhist."

Now, she said, she and her three siblings "don't know much about any particular religion and find it hard to see the value in other people's beliefs. . . . When people are against or for something in the name of religion, it's impossible for me to have any empathy at all for them."

Part of the temptation of silence is that many secularists are already adept at avoiding religion in their everyday lives. Almost 60 percent of the parents I surveyed said they had, at some point in their lives, avoided talking about their beliefs or refused to answer religious questions because they thought doing so would have brought them discomfort or shame; 41 percent said they felt the need to edit or hide parts of themselves from the people they love; and 35 percent said they had pretended to be religious by attending church, praying at dinner or baptizing a child, for example, just to satisfy the wishes or expectations of family members. When asked whether they were outspoken about their religious beliefs, 86 percent answered "somewhat," "occasionally," or "not at all"—indicating a clear hesitancy among most parents to share their beliefs openly.

Those of us who have spent our adult lives building walls around our lack of faith may not feel ready to tear down those walls, especially if it has the potential to lead to problems with our kid's teacher, or neighborhood buddy, or—God forbid—Grandma.

And it must be said that not all "avoiders" are doing so intentionally. Some of them *want* to talk to their kids about religion; they just don't know quite how to go about it.

"I wanted to be able to be straight with my kids," said a West Virginia mother whose two children are now grown. "But when it came right down to it, I didn't know quite what to say—so I usually said nothing."

Unfortunately, the consequences of silence are not limited to ignorance, embarrassment, and intolerance. Gaps in a child's cultural knowledge may become the proverbial vacuum that nature abhors, waiting to be filled with any number of errant ideas and, yes, even beliefs.

Ignoring religion can quickly turn religion into the elephant in the room—the child's room.

A Word about 'Religious Hijacking'

Austin Cline, once a regional director for the Council for Secular Humanism who writes about atheism and agnosticism for *about.com*, told me he was deeply concerned about the number of non-religious parents whose instincts are to gloss over the topic with their children.

"Avoiding discussions about religion is like avoiding discussions about sex," Cline said, totally stealing my metaphor from me. "The parent isn't made to feel uncomfortable, but the child is left on their own without rudder or guidance."

The most extreme cases, Cline said, involve situations in which children are dissatisfied with the guidance they're getting at home and go elsewhere for answers. Some children pick up religion from their friends and believe it without question; they may even venture into fundamentalist sects that jeopardize their physical or mental health.

Dale McGowan, co-author and editor of *Raising Freethinkers: A Practical Guide for Parenting Beyond Belief,* told me that he regularly talks with non-believing parents whose children join evangelist Christian groups or fundamentalist churches as teenagers. These parents come to him desperate for answers, wondering how such a thing could have happened when religion was never a topic of conversation in their families.

"That," McGowan always tells them, "is what you did wrong." Avoiding the topic of religion may make religion into something mysterious, and even enticing for some children. "It's the forbidden fruit," he said. "It's this thing that sort of freaks Mom and Dad out."

Angsty teenagers depressed about poor grades, unhappy with their friends, or uncertain about their places in the world may become especially susceptible to outside influences, when religion has never, or rarely, been discussed in their homes. All that some of them need is to be told the secret to happiness is behind Church Door Number 1; suddenly, they turn away from the practical support of their parents in favor of something completely different—a promise of something better, something bigger, something . . . supernatural.

McGowan calls this process "religious hijacking."

I love that term, and I'm quite sure it fits in some extreme cases; but in most families I suspect the phenomenon is less like a hijacking and more like a break-up. After all, whether you are a secular person separating from your parents' religious views or a religious person separating from your parents' secular views, the hurt is the same. Having been compatible for so long, one of you has decided to part spiritual ways.

Jennifer Austin grew up in Utah. Her mother was a non-practicing Mormon, her father a vocal opponent of Mormonism. She described her household as completely non-religious.

"My parents never spoke about religion, unless it was my father speaking poorly of the Mormons," Austin said. "We weren't raised attending church or saying prayers or speaking about God."

Today, Austin is a devout believer and member of the Church of Jesus Christ of Latter-Day Saints. She says her upbringing did nothing to keep her from becoming religious, and in fact there was a time when it just made her resentful.

"I used to worry that God would be angry with me," she said. "But it's okay because I learned (to believe) as an adult, and it's never too late."

Austin said her decision to embrace the LDS church was more about her relationship with a higher power than any perceived need for moral guidance. She said her parents "taught us to abide by the law, to treat others with respect, to appreciate people for who they are no matter their religion, age, gender or sexual preference." And, she said, after a few initial bumps, her relationship with her parents is now on solid ground.

As conversions go, Austin's was pretty darn benign, but many aren't. Sometimes it takes years for familial resentments to be settled—which is why, as non-religious parents, it's so important for us to meet our children's religious choices with support. When we don't, we risk contributing to yet another cycle of inter-generational tension surrounding matters of religious belief.

In 2012, KJ Dell'Antonia, author of the *New York Times' Motherlode* blog, wrote about the danger of not talking to children about race. In her essay, she said some parents assume not talking about race sends the message that race doesn't matter.

"But research suggests the opposite, that when we don't talk about race, our children continue to think about it—and what they think is that it matters too much to talk about."[12]

Avoiding religion can send the message that parents consider the entire subject to be scary, wrong or bad—in other words, too important even to talk about. Children may not grasp why religion is taboo in their households, but they may learn to respect their parents' silence. They may learn to keep their questions and feelings to themselves—or, at the very least, away from their parents.

The Wisconsin mom I quoted earlier—the one who doesn't discuss religion in her home? She went on to say this:

> *My daughter hears her friends [and] relatives talk about religion and tends to believe what they say. She clearly has*

questions about God and church and heaven, but is reluctant to have conversations with me about those things, despite our very open relationship about other topics. She wants to fit in with her peers, so is willing to accept what they say about religion rather than discuss with me what it is and what it means.

Some parents have told me that they don't wish to talk about religion in their secular homes because they don't want to make a big deal out of something that, to them, isn't a big deal.

"It's just not a very important subject," one parent said.

I asked McGowan about this. He said he sympathized with these parents, but pointed out that the question isn't whether religion is important to certain individuals, but whether it's important, period. And the answer, of course, is an unequivocal yes. Religion is worth talking about precisely because it's so important to so many people—people our children know and love.

Simply put, religion is everywhere we want to be. It's in our art and architecture, music and literature, plays, poetry and movies. It's steeped in our language, expressions, and clichés. It fills our history books and guides our politics. It's the reason we get our weekends off. It's on our money.

More broadly, religion is blamed for violence, wars, racism, sexism, child abuse, ritualistic killings, suicide cults, intolerance, hatred, and acts of terrorism. At the same time, it's credited with enormous acts of charity and goodwill, for bringing help to the desolate and meaning to the lost, for creating communities, reminding people of what's important in life, and for giving human beings hope, purpose, and joy. Even for those of us with no emotional attachments to faith, religion is an integral way of understanding our history, and of learning about and benefitting from the people in our lives. So, yes, religion is important.

To deny that is, in a way, to deny reality—an irony given that most secularists pride themselves on doing just the opposite.

When it comes to religion, there is sometimes a disconnect between wanting and doing. In an effort to protect children, we scare them. In an effort to teach them, we confuse them. In an effort to be honest with them, we indoctrinate them. Too often, kids are left to fend for themselves when it comes to understanding religion and religious people. They get glimpses of "the other side" but aren't able to see the big picture. And, as the world becomes more global, the big picture is mattering more and more.

One of the most unfortunate things I learned from Manning's study was that parents who take it upon themselves to provide religious guidance at home often fail. They don't necessarily know how to steer the discussions, she said, and quite often end up abandoning their efforts. Silence, again, becomes the reigning winner in the realm of non-religious parenting.

It doesn't have to be that way.

PART TWO *A New Direction*

CHAPTER THREE *Broaching the Subject*

When my daughter was two, and barely out of diapers, she had her first Potty Emergency. We'd been having lunch when suddenly she rose and sprinted to the bathroom with the speed and determination of a hunted deer. I'd been hopeful she made it in time, but when I arrived several seconds later, she was standing in front of the toilet, fully clothed, staring down at a puddle on the floor. Her little shoulders had fallen. Without looking up at me, she shook her head and said exactly what I would have said in the same situation:

"Jesus Christ."

I'm sure my Presbyterian ancestors would have been charmed to learn the only thing my daughter knew about the Christian messiah was that he made for an effective expletive.

In my home, and maybe yours, too, there weren't a lot of opportunities for religious references to arise outside of idioms, proverbs, and, frankly, the occasional profanity. We didn't attend a church, mosque, synagogue, or temple. We didn't pray before meals or emphasize the religious aspects of national holidays or have Bibles or Qur'ans lying around the house. God just didn't come up.

Sometimes, it seems, addressing religion with kids can seem so much easier when you have a particular religion to pass along. Very religious parents often know exactly what to say to their children because they are guided by the well-defined teachings of their faith—whether it be Buddhism, Hinduism, Judaism, Islam, Taoism, Sikhism, folk religions, or the great wide panoply of Christianity. For many, "good" and "bad" are defined for them. God is a given. Even death has a silver lining.

The challenge for those of us without a religious *ism*—or who simply wish for our children to think critically when it comes to religion—is knowing what to impart about issues of faith, and how. Sometimes we don't know how to kick things off, where to get started, and how young is *too* young.

When is the Right Time?

Lots of secular parents think religion is too complicated for young children to comprehend, and some worry that early exposure to religious ideas will bias children in one way or another. But waiting is a gamble. As we'll discuss later in the book, kids are capable of so much more than we give them credit for. And when we wait too long, we risk losing their interest altogether; religious literacy becomes a chore—for them and for us.

Precisely when and how you broach the subject with *your* child, though, will depend a lot on your child's personality, not to mention your own worldview, the community in which you live, and the sorts of beliefs your child is most likely to encounter in talks with her peers. But, for purposes of planning, count on kicking things off around kindergarten. If you wait a little longer, that's fine. But do keep in mind that the longer you wait, the harder the transition is likely to be. By eight, your child will probably have picked up a lot of things from peers; he might even be worried about what he's hearing, or feel an inexplicable lack of belonging.

Here are some general guidelines.

Ages Four to Six. At this age, most kids are ready to start exploring ideas of spirituality. This is when blossoming imaginations begin welcoming supernatural ideas and when concepts like "good" and "evil" come into focus. It's around this time, too, when inquisition replaces demand as the rhetorical tool of choice: "Why did this happen?" "What happens if someone does that?" "Why?" Around five, most children are being exposed to the reality that Mom and Dad don't have exclusive control of the thought process: Kids at school also have ideas to share.

Ages Seven and Eight. If, by the time your kid turns seven or eight, you have made clear that faith is a subject you are open to discussing, you ought to hear the subject come up naturally from time to time. Your child will likely enjoy thinking about how the world was made and how humans came to be. (Evolution fascinates children of this age.) They may want to discuss what they believe in comparison to what others believe and may surprise you with the depth of their thoughts on the matter. (If you are a believer, don't forget to talk about non-belief, as well!) Talk a little about the belief systems of your extended family. Encourage your kids to share their own thoughts, whatever they may be. And don't worry about distinguishing between religions at this early stage. Try pointing out what all religions have in common, rather than what sets them apart. All religions, for instance, have sacred texts. All have life-cycle celebrations. All have views of the afterlife. All have holiday celebrations. Once they grasp that, you can individualize religions a bit more.

Ages Nine to Eleven. At this point, religious talks will become commonplace. Expand on their knowledge. Work religious literacy into your conversations. Discuss some of the basic differences in religions (see the appendix for my *Cheat Sheet to World Religions*) and how those differences sometimes lead to conflict. Discussions about "God's will" versus "free will" are age-appropriate at this stage. Look for opportunities to point out real-world examples of religion—in books and architecture and clothing, for example. Take advantage of religious symbols in your community, lyrics in music, biblical clichés in your speech. Consider "celebrating" various religious holidays. (You'll find loads more information on this front in *Chapter Seven: Kickstarting Religious Literacy*, as well as in the appendix.) If your child enjoys more philosophical discussions, you might find it fun to ask kids the question teacher Jim Morrison asks kids in his high school classroom: "Did God create man, or did man create God?"

Ages Twelve and Thirteen. Depending on the child, you may be nearing the end of your influence, to a certain extent. As your child gets to be a teenager, she will likely begin to turn away from you and instead look to her friends for guidance and direction. That said, this is also the time when her critical thinking skills kick into high gear. Kids enjoy exploring the psychological and political aspects of religion more deeply at this age. Your talks might become increasingly more casual and unfiltered. Good! Just be sure to emphasize how much you value diversity and tolerance. Explain that religion is as much about culture as beliefs and that it's important not to like or dislike people based on their religion or skin color or sexual orientation or any other identifying feature that makes them different. Sometimes those who are the most different from us have the most to offer us.

'FACT, FICTION OR BELIEF?'

If you're not sure your child is "ready" to discuss religious belief, try playing a game called "Fact, Fiction or Belief" to find out for sure. Define *fact* as anything that's true; *fiction* as anything that's made up; and *belief* as anything that some people think is fact and other people think is fiction. (For purposes of this game, all opinions, preferences, and tastes can be considered *belief*.) Then make statements and have your child label them accordingly. For instance, you might say: "The moon is in the sky." (*Fact*!) "You like to eat rocks." (*Fiction*!) "Pink is the best of all the colors." (*Belief*!) Remember: Don't try to make things too literal or complicated, or to inject actual religious beliefs into your examples. Just keep in mind the point of the game—to see if your child can grasp the concept of belief—and have fun with it.

Simple Words, Neutral Tone

So now that you know when to start, let's talk about how.

First of all, there's what you say and then there's how you say it. Attitude is important. If you keep your shoulders stiff and your voice low and you occasionally clench your teeth and sigh deeply during these talks, your kid is going to get the message pretty quickly that this is a subject that's best avoided.

So keep your tone in check. Let your child know that you are not passing judgment on the world around you; you're merely an interested observer. Share your personal beliefs with a certain amount of dispassion. There are no disastrous consequences (i.e., hell) if your child chooses "incorrectly." So take your dog out of the fight. Present information in the most straightforward way you can, and let your kid decide what to do (or not do) with the information.

Todd Parr, a children's book author and illustrator, is great at this. Parr's work emphasizes inclusiveness, diversity, and self-confidence. His writing is sweet and kind, his illustrations vibrant and kid-like. In his first book, *The Okay Book*, he writes: "It's okay to be short/ It's okay to be tall/ It's okay to wear two different socks/ It's okay to have freckles."[13]

Parr's approach can easily be adopted when talking about religion with kids. "It's okay for people to believe and behave in different ways" is a wonderful thought-gift for a kid.

Of course, before you get into beliefs, you first must be relatively sure your child understands what the word means. With kids, it may be simpler to describe a belief as *anything that some people think is true and others do not think is true*. You might explain that people have beliefs about friends, about school, about lots of different things; people also have beliefs about how the world was made, why people should be nice to each other, and what happens after we die.

If you're not the type of person who speaks well "on the fly," you might try writing down some talking points using open, neutral language. Like this:

Some people believe everything in the world was created by a being called God.

Some people believe God watches over them and keeps them safe.

Some people believe God helps them make good decisions.

Some people believe God answers their prayers.

Some people have different names for God: Allah, Jehovah, Brahman . . .

Some people believe there are many gods.

Some people believe books written a long time ago tell true stories about God.

Some people believe God has chosen certain human beings to talk to. (They call these people prophets.)

Some people believe prophets are important to God and should be important to us.

Some people believe in some prophets but not in others. Some people do not believe in prophets.

Some people believe when they die, they will see God for the first time in a place often called heaven or paradise.

Some people believe that only those who believe in God go to heaven.

Some people believe that after they die, they will be born again as different people, or even animals.

Some people believe that there is no more life after we die, but that death is peaceful because it makes us just like we were before we were born.

Some people believe God may not be real.

Some people believe God is definitely not real.

Some people aren't sure what to believe.

Some people believe it's very important to believe in God.

Some people believe it's not at all important to believe in God.

Then you might talk to your child about what it means to be kind to other people, despite what they do or do not believe, that diversity of thought makes the world more interesting, and that you are a family that values all people, regardless of their faith.

I offer one side note to this subject of simplicity. The younger the child, the less you should talk. They will undoubtedly lose interest, and—frankly—their curiosity probably only extends so far. For example, if your three-year-old asks, out of the blue, "What is an angel?" he's probably not asking for an essay on everything you know about angels. He wants the short answer.

"An angel," you might say, "is like a fairy with wings."

At five or six, your child might be ready for a few additional details: "Some people think that really good people become angels after they die."

Only later—at, say, eight or nine—will kids appreciate a more sophisticated answer. But, even then, remember to keep it simple: "Lots of religions believe in angels, which are usually depicted as caring, human-like spirits with feathered wings who float between heaven and Earth. They are said to watch over people to keep them safe, which is why you might sometimes hear the term 'guardian angel.'"

RECOMMENDED READING

Really, Really Big Questions about God, Faith and Religion

Written by British philosopher Julian Baggini, *Really, Really Big Questions about God, Faith and Religion* is a great book for kids ages eight to twelve, who are ready to explore religious issues in a little more depth. Each section of the book begins with a question. They include: *Can we criticize religion? Should we fear God? Why do people worship? What if there is no God? Does religion cause wars? Do I have a soul?* Great questions, right? The answers are equally compelling, mostly because Baggini writes from a perspective that is, as he put it to me, "basically, genuinely open-minded." Baggini constantly urges children to make up their own minds about how to answer these questions and what to believe. And he makes clear those who don't believe in any religious notions can live perfectly happy, fulfilling lives—just like those who do.

Answering the Big Questions

What you choose to share about religion, and in what way, will give your kid certain coordinates from which to form an opinion. This is part of why being honest with kids about what you believe is essential. So before you start discussing faith issues, think through some basic questions on your own: Do you believe in God? Do you believe in an afterlife? Do you believe humanity has a purpose? Are you satisfied with your beliefs?

Is the way you answer these questions for yourself different than how you would answer them for your child? And, if so, why?

When we hide beliefs from our kids, we may think we are protecting our kids from confusion, hurt, or undue influence; but far more often we are protecting ourselves from awkwardness, guilt, or embarrassment. And, in doing so, we risk cracking the foundation of a strong, trusting relationship with the people who matter to us the most: our children.

A friend's son once surprised her by asking if it was true that "God died on the cross." She clarified that it was Jesus who "died on a cross," and that some people believe Jesus was the son of God. Her son then asked if she believed that. "I don't want to tell you what I believe," she said, "because I want you to make up your own mind."

Indoctrination is not a byproduct of simple honesty or exposure. Telling your child what you believe, or exposing them to what others believe, will not indoctrinate them. Instead, it will show your willingness to be open and forthcoming. It will show them that there is no shame in sharing one's beliefs with others. And it will show them that yours is a household that talks openly and respectfully about tough subjects—including faith.

Below are some ideas about how you could answer the more common childhood questions. Just be sure that, before you use these answers, you think through them on your own and make sure they feel right to you. There is nothing to memorize here, so play this your own way. Tweak as necessary. Ask questions yourself. Show your kid you are interested in what she thinks. Admit you don't know everything. And, remember, brevity is your friend.

What is God?

"God is a word that a lot of people use to mean different things. Many people think of God as an invisible being who made everything in the world. Some people think God watches over them from the sky and helps them to be good. Some people think God is just a part of our imaginations, like a dream."

What does God look like?

"People who believe in God have lots of different ideas about that. Some people think God looks like an old man. Others think of the sky, or the stars, or the goodness in people. Others think of nature. Do you have a picture of God in your mind? What does it look like?"

Is God real?

"No one knows for sure, but many people think so. Even though they can't see God, they believe in him, and that is called faith. Not everyone has faith, but lots of people do. It's okay to believe in God, and it's okay not to believe in God."

Do you believe in God?

If you believe in God, say, "I do." If you don't believe in God, say, "I don't." If you have an undefined spiritual sense, say so. ("I believe in something that connects us all together, but I don't call it God.") And if you don't know what you believe, don't be afraid to say that, too. It's perfectly acceptable to not have all the answers when it comes to religion; just be sure that whatever answer you give is the truthful one.

Why do you believe that?

"I have been thinking about it for a long time—years and years. And you'll probably think about it for a long time, too. You will grow up and learn new things and you will decide what makes sense to you. You may change your mind a lot, too—lots of people do—or you might always believe what you believe now."

What is religion?

"Religion is a collections of beliefs, as well as views about how people ought to behave. Some religions involve God or gods, and some don't. Religion has been around for thousands of years. Many religions have gone away with time, and many others have kept going. Some religions were formed very recently."

Do I have to believe in God to be good?

"No. No one needs God to be a good person, just as they don't need God to feel comfort or to have a full and satisfying life. Being a good person means being kind and treating others the way you want to be treated."

Are some religions bad?

"Religion isn't bad or good, although it can seem that way sometimes. Some people do good things for their religions; and some people do bad things for their religions. If you are mean to people just because they are different from you—because of religion or for any reason—that is bad. Hurting people is wrong, whether you are religious or not."

What is the difference between spiritual and religious?

"*Spiritual* means believing that there is something more to the world than what we can see. *Religious* means having a specific set of beliefs, rituals, and celebrations—usually based on very old books."

Can you be religious and not have supernatural beliefs?

"Yes. Buddhism is a religion that often involves supernatural beliefs, but does not *require* them. (Buddha, remember, was just a regular man who had some good ideas about how to live.) Also, many people belong to churches or temples or mosques because they like the community and the culture of those places, but they do not believe in the supernatural stuff."

Why are we talking about this?

"Religion is something that matters to a lot of people. I talk to you about it so that you can make up your own mind about what you believe, and because I want you to be able to understand and appreciate all the different people you are going to meet during your life. Knowledge, awareness, and curiosity are traits that tend to invite new and positive experiences. In short, I think teaching you a bit about religion will help make you a smarter, friendlier, and happier person."

Can I talk about my beliefs in school?

"Of course. You can talk about your beliefs anywhere. But you should know that people often feel strongly about their beliefs—so strongly that it can lead to disagreements and hurt feelings, which is why you probably won't learn much about it in school and why some people encourage children not to talk about it on the playground."

Is it okay for me to believe what Grandma believes?

"It is okay to believe anything you want, as long as it doesn't hurt people and as long as you don't feel pressured to believe it. When someone pressures you by saying, 'I won't be your friend anymore' or 'You have to believe this, or something bad will happen to you'—that is not okay. People can tell you what they believe, but they shouldn't tell you what to believe yourself. And you shouldn't tell them, either."

Where did we come from?

"The entire universe—everything we see (and what we don't) started 13.8 billion years ago. The universe has been expanding ever since, and is still expanding. To this day, scientists are still trying to figure out how it all happened, and why. In the meantime, some people believe God created the universe, while others believe it happened by itself."

FROM THE BLOG

'God Wears a Green Shirt'

When my husband and I started talking with our daughter about religion, we didn't mention the word "religion." It was all about "God." Whenever we told her religious stories—whether they came from Hindu mythology or from the Bible—they would fall under the same category: "God Stories." Maxine loved to hear God Stories, and to ponder the existence of God. Some days, she believed. Others, she didn't. Once, when she came back from a trip to her paternal grandparents' house, she and her dad struck up a conversation about it—which I proceeded to record on my phone. She was five. Here's how it went.

Maxine: I believe in God. And Nana believes in God.

Charlie: Why do you believe in God?

Maxine: I know what he looks like. I'll tell you what he looks like. He has a very white, long beard that reaches up to heaven. He has a green shirt.

Charlie: A T-shirt? Or a shirt with a collar?

Maxine: Actually it's a red shirt and green jeans. Nobody believes this, but he's bigger than the clouds. He can fly.

Charlie: Cool!

Maxine: When people prayer, they're actually talking to God.

Charlie: When they *pray*, what do they say?

Maxine: 'Dear God, I want you to give me a little pail' . . . like that.

Charlie: So they are asking for things?

Maxine: Yes.

Charlie: Cool! And do they say 'Thank you'?

Maxine: Yes.

Charlie: Great.

Maxine: NOW do you believe in God?

Charlie: No, I really don't believe in God. But that's okay.

Maxine: He's invisible.

Charlie: So you can't see him?

Maxine: He's bigger than the sky.

Charlie: Do you know what it's called when you believe in something but you can't see it?

Maxine: What?

Charlie: Faith. And do you know why some people believe in God?

Maxine: Why?

Charlie: They believe that God takes care of you.

Maxine: (Nodding) They believe God made our babies. God made us. God made the clouds. God made the sky. God made the sun. Everything in the whole wide world. Even wood. Even seeds.

[Pause.]

Maxine: This is in the olden days, when Papa was first born.

Religion isn't rocket science. You know much of what you need to know already, and you can learn the rest relatively easily. And don't worry if you screw up from time to time; that goes with the territory. Luckily, kids aren't going to remember precisely what you said as much as they'll remember the overall message. They're not as focused on your words as your attitude, your demeanor and your comfort level. So take a stab at it. Start some conversations. Get some practice. Soon I think you'll find that talking about religion is a hell of a lot easier than *not* talking about it.

CHAPTER FOUR *Giving Kids a Choice —and Meaning It*

I'm fairly confident that, if you're reading this book, you are at least somewhat turned off by the idea of indoctrination. Non-religious parents usually are. In my survey, nine out of ten parents said it was important to them that their kids came to their own, independent conclusions about religion, faith, and belief. Regardless of their own worldviews, these parents wanted their kids to choose their own religious (or non-religious) identities for themselves.

Said one parent: "I want them to seek knowledge and arrive at their own conclusions with minimal influence from either side—me included."

"I don't want to brainwash my kids with my own views," said another. "I want them to decide for themselves what they believe."

"Belief should not be imposed," said a third. "It should be explored and constantly re-evaluated."

Indeed, at its most successful, indoctrination takes advantage of children's undeveloped brains—teaching kids what to think, rather than how to think; treating belief as indistinguishable from fact; and suggesting that bad things await those who believe outside the norm. All this carries the potential to lower a child's self-esteem, self-confidence and self-worth—the very attributes that enable children to resist peer pressure and make good decisions through their adolescence and beyond.

Yet, despite such strong statements against indoctrination and in favor of choice, only 16 percent of the parents I surveyed said they could "support their children 100 percent" if they chose religious beliefs different from their own.

That's not to say they would throw their kids out into the cold. Far from it. Thirteen percent said they'd be disappointed but "supportive on the outside," 22 percent said they'd speak their minds but try to respect their children's decisions, and 37 percent it would depend entirely on the specific religious beliefs; the more conservative the religion, the more they would struggle to support their children.

It's easy to see the conflict. We don't want to indoctrinate our kids, but we don't want to lose them to closed-minded fundamentalists either. We want our kids to choose their own beliefs, but only within reason.

Letting Kids Choose Their Clothes (And Their Faith)

When Maxine was still an infant, my husband and I took her to a local coffee shop for breakfast. At the booth over was an early-30s couple, each with multiple tattoos and piercings and jet-black hair to match their clothes. I wouldn't have paid much attention to the couple except for the company they kept. Across from them sat their daughter, who was around six and dressed head-to-toe in pink. Along with a pretty dress and fancy shoes, the girl wore a shimmering headband to hold back her long mane of perfectly combed, blond hair.

As the family stood up to leave, it was impossible not to notice: These two Morrissey types had given birth to a Barbie doll. The mother caught me mid-smile, and smiled back. "All she wears is pink," she told me. "I buy her all these black T-shirts, but she won't touch any of them."

After they left, I thought: *I love that little family*. And now, all these years later, I still do.

There is something I viscerally respond to when parents don't push their children to become mini-mes, when they let their children's individuality outweigh their own personal preferences, or even embarrassment. Giving children information and encouraging kids to be true to themselves and aware of their own abilities; to make their own decisions and mistakes; and to value their own unique perspectives on the world—that is such a wonderful thing to do for a child. It may not always be easy for us in the moment, but we are guaranteed to see the payoff for decades to come.

My reaction to that family was the same one I experienced many years later when I read a sweet, moving, and incredibly supportive wedding speech written by the father of a lesbian bride. Before toasting his daughter and his daughter's new wife, the father, Stewart Middler, said this:

"I've been under the impression for years that it was the honor and duty for the father of the bride to give his daughter in matrimony to her beloved. I take that as my right and my privilege. I do it with the greatest joy and deepest love."

Our ability to embrace every part of our children is the true test of our unconditional love. We are proving to them that we want to support them on their life journeys—not just drag them behind us on ours.

Young children are vulnerable little creatures. So much of their world comes down to "I like" and "I don't like," "I want" and "I don't want." From early ages, telling them that what they like or want is wrong can send the message that they aren't smart enough or that they make bad decisions. And we all know the damage that can do to a person.

Insecurity is something that children (and adults) suffer quietly and alone. Every time we undercut our kids' individuality, or impose our own opinions as Almighty Fact, or make them feel bad for having faith (or doubt) in what other people say, we put their self-confidence at risk.

When my child got old enough to dress herself, I understood all too well the plight of the hipsters in the coffee shop. Sometimes I felt the tug of opposition when we were out shopping and Maxine gravitated toward the bright, almost florescent, prom-style dresses that looked like they'd been bedazzled by Cher.

But I did try very hard to support her choices. Because letting kids dress in the clothes that make them feel good is the right thing to do. By allowing our children to choose what they like, we are affirming that their opinions are valid, that their taste is respected, that their choices are worthy. We are telling them it's better than okay to be who they are; it's wonderful.

We Can't Choose Facts . . . Or Can We?

As parents, we can't help but want to influence the direction of our children's lives. After all, we have lived more years than they have, have known more people, and have experienced more things. We have wisdom to impart, and sometimes we feel a duty to bestow that wisdom upon our kids. We also want to keep our kids safe, and sometimes that means keeping them close to us—physically, emotionally, mentally, and, yes, spiritually.

But if we're being honest, we must admit that at least part of our desire to keep our kids close to us is inherently selfish. When our children turn away and head in another direction, it's a blow to our egos. It can feel like another way of saying: "You don't know best after all" or, even worse, "I don't want to be like you." That can sting.

Parents are especially susceptible to the sting of rejection if their children have accepted beliefs that the parents hold to be ridiculous in some way. A great number of science-oriented parents I know have an especially hard time with this. Sure, they understand how people might "choose faith," but that doesn't mean they get to "choose facts." Facts are facts.

"I don't want to discourage my kid's honest exploration of his beliefs," one parent told me, but "I can't pretend to be open-minded about this."

As a non-believer myself, I can relate. After Charlie and I had decided to let Maxine choose for herself what to believe about God and religion, a family member pressed me on the possibility that Maxine might end up getting everything wrong.

"You don't believe in God," he said. "Wouldn't letting her believe in God be the same as letting her believe that the world is flat?"

At first, I admit, that's exactly what I thought. (Thus, my goofy reaction the first time Maxine brought the whole thing up.) But over time, I realized that I wasn't giving my kid enough credit. It's my daughter's mind, not mine, that creates her truth. And if I didn't give her the freedom to accept or reject facts, I wouldn't be trusting her ability to think critically or giving her the freedom to practice her skills in that area.

Does this mean that we don't have a duty to tell our kids facts? Or that we need to be so sensitive to religion that we put creationism and evolution on the same level? Not at all! Absolutely tell your child about how the world works. Tell him everything you know about science. But then allow him to do with that information what he likes.

Getting back to the earlier question: It would be weird and quite puzzling if, knowing all she does about the Earth, Maxine had chosen to believe the world was flat. But there would have been no reason to stress over it, either. That particular belief doesn't hurt anyone.

Some parents will struggle with this piece of advice more than others. One survey respondent told me, "Our job is to teach [children] truth, not lies and make-believe stories. When kids grow up and can drive, drink, think for themselves, they can explore their own freedom of thought."

So let me throw one more thought out there—one that might speak more directly to those who struggle with the fear that their kids will someday choose to believe things that are not factual. We often hear that children will model our behavior, and that's true. But a lesser-known truth in childhood development is that our children often expect to be treated in adulthood the way they were treated as children. That is, if we treat them well, they will naturally gravitate toward people in life who also will treat them well. If we bully them or demand they behave in certain ways, they may well seek out people in life who bully them or demand they behave in certain ways. In other words, we are creating their "normal," and children will for the rest of their lives, unconsciously or consciously, seek out what feels normal to them.

What I'm saying is that allowing our kids religious freedom at home by honoring their own thought process makes it far more likely that they will exercise their own religious freedom later in the presence of *others*. Likewise, closing the valve on your child's religious freedom by insisting that God is a myth may make it easier for others to assume control of that valve down the road.

The goal should not be to insist on a set of truths, but to put your child in charge of his own truth.

Now, at this point, you might wonder how you can be entirely honest about your worldviews while still giving your kids a choice. What if your honest answers to your child's questions make religious people sound downright nutty? Should you share those views, too? And wouldn't it be dishonest not to?

Editing our innermost thoughts is not lying; it's being selective about which thoughts we share. And being selective, especially when it comes to bias and prejudice, is a parental necessity. We'll get into this more in later chapters, but for now, just remember to use discretion, and speak in age-appropriate ways.

It's also worth mentioning here that, for whatever reason, some people (and kids) are more inquisitive and skeptical than others. In children who are "natural believers"—generally accepting what they are told at face value—indoctrination (by you or other people) is more likely to occur. So be aware. Know your kid. Watch your language.

For example, when talking about the more irrational aspects of religion, don't just roll your eyes and wave it off as "absurd." Instead, explain: "Some religious people are happy in their religion and don't care if their beliefs go against what we know to be true about the world."

Remember, if your honesty requires you to make nasty judgments about groups of people or disparage the intelligence or worth of individuals based solely on their religious affiliations, you're getting into indoctrination territory, and it's time to change the subject.

Or better yet, work on changing yourself.

Measuring the Space Between Indoctrination and Brainwashing

Admittedly, it's much easier to give a message of free will to children when you're not up against other forces. If you believe your children are very likely to be greeted by indoctrination techniques from family members with far different ideas than your own, it will be harder to throw open the door and allow your kid carte blanche to choose a belief system that feels right to them.

But that's all the more reason to understand a little bit more about indoctrination—what it is, and what it isn't. Earlier we defined indoctrination as *teaching children that your way is the only right way to believe and that people who disagree with these beliefs are less moral, less intelligent and less worthy of respect*. But it's also important to understand that, despite how people use the word colloquially, *indoctrination* differs greatly from *brainwashing*.

True brainwashing is mind control, also known as thought reform, and it involves unethically manipulative methods of persuasion. Robert Jay Lifton, an American psychiatrist, has devoted his life to the study of mind control. His books include *The Nazi Doctors; Cults in Our Midst: The Hidden Menace in Our Everyday Lives;* and *Thought Reform and the Psychology of Totalism: A Study of 'Brainwashing' in China*. In the latter, Lifton lays out "Eight Criteria for Thought Reform."[14]

They are:

Milieu Control. The control of information and communication, resulting in extreme isolation from the outside world.

Mystical Manipulation. Experiences that appear spontaneous but are actually planned and orchestrated to demonstrate divine authority, spiritual advancement, or other insight.

Demand for Purity. The requirement to conform to the ideology of the group and strive for perfection. Guilt and shame are often employed.

Confession. Ways to monitor the personal thoughts ("sins") of individual members—which are then discussed and exploited by group leaders.

Sacred Science. The idea that the group's ideology is beyond questioning or dispute.

Loading the Language. The use of jargon and terminology that the outside world does not understand as a means of gaining thought-control and conformity.

Doctrine over Person. Subordinating all personal experiences to the ideology of the group.

Dispensing of Existence. In order to be saved or enlightened, individuals must convert to the group's ideology. If they are critical of the group, or decide to leave the group, they are rejected by all members.

It's clear that, under Lifton's criteria, there is a significant difference between what happens to children in, say, Hebrew School or Catholic Catechism classes, and what happens to the character of Karl in Anthony Burgess' *A Clockwork Orange*. Religious people may be employing one or two (or three) of the above methods. I know quite a few Catholics very familiar with number three, and a few Muslims familiar with number seven, and some Mormons familiar with number eight, and, oh my God, can we talk about the broad employment of number five?!—but certainly not all.

I do not mean to minimize the effects of indoctrination, but we don't do our kids any favors by exaggerating the concept, either. Our children should be able to differentiate between what goes on within most mainstream religions and what goes on within most religious cults.

It's also important to understand that there are many reasons religious people indoctrinate their kids.

Here are twelve of them.

Comfort. The idea of heaven can be undeniably comforting, especially to children with anxieties about death or dying. By instilling children with belief in an afterlife, parents may feel they are protecting them from existential pain. And, indeed, in the short-term at least, they might be right.

Calling. Those who feel they've been "called" by God to fulfill a duty may see it as their divine obligation to bring children into their faith.

Community. Parents who derive a sense of belonging from their religious community may deem it in their children's best interest to be members of that community, too.

Tribalism. Parents may indoctrinate their children because they don't want their "tribe" to die out. Their children's membership is required to keep the religion going year after year.

Fear. Devoutly religious parents who believe in hellfire and damnation will indoctrinate, in whole or in part, out of concern for their children's eternal well-being.

Ignorance. Sometimes the blind lead the blind. Those who have been brought up to believe a certain way *just because* may not think twice before doing the same thing with their kids.

Morals. Despite evidence to the contrary, many people still believe there is a necessary connection between religion and moral acts.[15] Parents who have been brought up in a religious household may not know how to instill morals without the aid of religion.

Parenting Style. Parents with authoritarian parenting styles are likely to demand certain behaviors of their children, and this bleeds over into the religious arena. Kids may be expected to obey God, just as they are expected to obey Mom and Dad.

Politics. Those whose religion is completely wrapped up in their politics may indoctrinate their kids as a means to an end.

Protection. Places of worship can be safe havens from the less desirable sides of the youth experience: early sex, drugs, alcohol. Getting children involved in a religious community can be a parent's attempt to stave off those things.

Tradition. For some families, religion acts as an heirloom—something of personal value handed down from one generation to the next. In these cases, the truth of supernatural beliefs may be inconsequential. Religion provides a structure for family get-togethers, a way to pass on memories, and a vehicle to understand one another.

Truth. When parents believe they possess the "truth" about the universe, they may think that the wisdom of their own life journeys *must* inform the beliefs of their children.

Parents who indoctrinate their kids into a religion are probably living their lives the best way they know how. We may not always agree with their choices; but it may help us to understand their motives. It may help us to understand ours, too.

RECOMMENDED READING
No! That's Wrong!

Religion is more about feelings than facts. Beliefs that you may think are silly or stupid or embarrassing or sad or flat-out wrong may make perfect sense in someone else's brain. *No! That's Wrong!*, by Zhaohua Ji and Cui Xu, makes this point beautifully. Originally published in Chinese, the book tells the tale of a bunny who finds a pair of underpants blowing in the wind and determines they must be a hat. After all, his ears fit perfectly through the little leg holes. We, the readers, keep telling him "No! That's wrong! They're underpants!" But the bunny is thrilled with his find, and proceeds to hop around the animal kingdom, where his friends comment on what a marvelous hat he's wearing. But, of course, the bunny has underpants on his head. Finally, under peer pressure from us, the readers—we're such jerks!—our little bunny friend puts the underpants on correctly. His tail doesn't fit, and the underpants are uncomfortable. After getting feedback from his friends and looking at himself in the glassy surface of a lake, the bunny takes off the underpants and puts them back on his head. "No, I was right!" he says, hopping merrily along. "It's a wonderful hat!"

FROM THE BLOG
Coolest. Mom. Ever.

In mid-October 2012, I was standing under a shade tree in front of my kid's kindergarten classroom, waiting for class to be dismissed and chatting with one of the other moms, whose name is, for the purposes of this story at least, Loren. At some point during our chat, Loren mentioned to me, sort of off-handedly, that her five-year-old, Justin, had become obsessed with learning Mandarin.

Finding that rather unusual, I asked for the back story.

The previous August, she told me, Justin had been in a swimming class with a few other children, including a Chinese-American girl, whom he had befriended. As the classes drew to a close, the little girl's mom invited Justin to join their church's Vacation Bible School. Justin desperately wanted to go with his new friend, so Loren agreed to check it out.

Unbeknownst to either of them, however, the church in question turned out to be a Chinese Baptist church full of Chinese Baptist people. And about the time Loren began wondering whether this was really the best fit for Justin, the little boy was being happily ushered off to his first activity.

Now, let me say this: Neither Loren nor her husband are particularly religious. He was raised Catholic, but isn't practicing. She considers herself somewhat non-religious, having been raised in a family that, as she put it, "changed religions like underwear."

But here was Justin, attending a Chinese Baptist church—and loving every minute of it. In fact, he was so taken with the whole thing that, once Vacation Bible School ended, he asked to be enrolled in the church's Youth Ministry class *and* its Sunday School class, and insisted the whole family attend the church's weekly sermon and luncheon. All told, Justin would be committing three and half hours of every Sunday to the Chinese Baptists.

Did I mention that this family already had a lot going on? Justin had two younger siblings: a very active three-year-old brother and a baby sister with Down Syndrome.

And did I also mention that, while the lunch was comprised of a mouth-watering assortment of Chinese food, the sermons themselves were sometimes in Mandarin with really shitty English translation?

"We're the only ones in the whole congregation who aren't Chinese," Loren said, and then laughed. "It's tough. It's tough."

"How often do you go?" I asked.

"Every Sunday," she said. "Every Sunday since August."

And that's when I knew.

"You," I said, "are the coolest mom ever."

My sister is fond of this one monologue in the movie *Lars and the Real Girl*, in which Lars, who is in love with an anatomically correct sex doll named Bianca, is confronted by his sister-in-law.

"Every person in this town bends over backward to make Bianca feel at home," the sister-in-law says. "Why do you think she has so many places to go and so much to do? Because of you! Because all these people love *you*! We push her wheelchair. We drive her to work. We drive her home. We wash her. We dress her. We get her up, and put her to bed. We carry her. And she is not petite, Lars. Bianca is a big, big girl! None of this is easy for any of us, but we do it. We do it for *you*."

Now, I readily acknowledge that a Chinese Baptist church is not the same as a mail-order whore doll. Nor is Justin at all similar to a deeply troubled but affable 30-year-old. But still. The sweetness is the same—

because both situations answer the same question: How far would you go to actively support the happiness of someone you love, even if you don't fully understand it yourself?

Every single Sunday this couple with so much going on, dressed up their children, and themselves, and marched off to listen to an hour-plus-long sermon they didn't always understand, eat lunch with people they didn't know, and celebrate a faith that wasn't theirs.

None of this was easy for any of them, but they did it. They did it for Justin. They did it because they love Justin.

Postscript: *Not long ago I ran into Loren and asked her whether she was still attending the Chinese Baptist church. She said no, that they had finally stopped after about a year. "Why?" I asked. "Justin just didn't want to go anymore," she said. "I think he eventually got sick of eating Chinese."*

Giving your child the freedom to choose his own beliefs may feel awkward to you at times, but it shouldn't. The bet that you make—that your child will eventually come around to your way of thinking—is a pretty safe one. Children are predisposed to believe the way you do. You set the tone for the rest of their lives, and it takes more effort for your child to reject your beliefs than to accept them. If you are kind and respectful, and you have told your child what you believe and why (without indoctrinating him), it is highly likely he'll grow up to view the world in about the same, logical way that you do.

But if he doesn't—if he becomes a Methodist or Buddhist, for example—he will still be your friend and will treat you with respect because you have taught him, by example, to respect others for who they are. And this same respect for others will steer him away from radical groups that hate, demonize, and even kill those who disagree with them.

So relax. There is nothing to be afraid of if you approach the subject with empathy, not fear. Think of religion as a learning tool, not a brainwashing tool. And know that you can be completely honest with your children while at the same time taking a step back and letting them absorb as many other points of view as they can.

CHAPTER FIVE *Teaching Tolerance (Or: How Not to Be a Dick)*

All but the zealots among us want our kids to be tolerant of other human beings. It's sort of the minimum standard of our time. We don't have to love one another, but we must, at the very least, tolerate them.

But what does that even mean anyway?

Religious tolerance is a tricky concept—not just because of the wide range of definitions people attach to it, but because we don't all agree that "tolerance" should be the goal. A man eats a piece of rancid beef but is able to tolerate it; in other words, he doesn't vomit. A woman tolerates an abusive husband; she hates him but is terrified to the point of inaction.

You can see why some people would wish to aspire a bit higher.

On the other hand, some anti-religious people believe tolerance is too generous a concept when it comes to religion—that tolerating harmful, religious-based views is part of the problem with our society. What we need to do, they argue, is reject religion outright.

When I asked non-religious parents to define what "religious tolerance" meant to them, the answers were, understandably, all over the place. Here's what I mean.

> *Tolerance means acknowledging religious beliefs.*
>
> *Tolerance means that everyone should have freedom of conscience but not the 'freedom' to impose their beliefs on others.*
>
> *Tolerance means you leave me alone and I'll leave you alone. That includes lawmaking.*
>
> *Tolerance means that people are allowed to have their own religious beliefs but that those who do not share them are also allowed to openly discuss, mock, and point out its absurdity. I don't think tolerance means that we have to stand by idly and let others' religions be forced on us or shut our mouths in the company of those who put their views out there.*

I think 'tolerance' is a meaningless, overused word best reserved for describing how one should deal with unruly children in public.

I hate the word 'tolerance' and don't understand why it's used so often and so positively. I know it's supposed to be a good thing, but can you imagine how you'd feel if someone you liked said that they tolerated you?

I have to think about this.

What Tolerance Means in Practice

D'Arcy Lyness, a child and adolescent psychologist and the behavioral health editor for a website called *KidsHealth*, defines tolerance as an attitude of openness and respect for the differences that exist among people. She goes on to say:

> *Tolerance means respecting and learning from others, valuing differences, bridging cultural gaps, rejecting unfair stereotypes, discovering common ground, and creating new bonds. Tolerance, in many ways, is the opposite of prejudice. Does tolerance mean that all behaviors have to be accepted? Of course not. Behaviors that disrespect or hurt others, like being mean or bullying, or behaviors that break social rules, like lying or stealing, should not be tolerated. Tolerance is about accepting people for who they are—not about accepting bad behavior. Tolerance also means treating others the way you would like to be treated.*[16]

There is a difference between respecting religious people and respecting religious beliefs, and advice columnist Richard Wade is a master of making this distinction. Wade's column runs regularly on the *Friendly Atheist* website, where he is considered a godsend—or the secular equivalent of a godsend—to thousands of people struggling with the sometimes painful intersection of belief and non-belief.

In October 2010, a mother wrote to Wade about how her son had learned, from her in-law's church, that "evolution is a lie."

"I am having a really, really hard time balancing my worldview with that of my in-laws without insulting the one they hear in this church," said the mother, who wrote in anonymously. "I don't want my kids to think less of these people, but how do I do that when the [preacher] stands up there and spouts ignorance at them?"[17]

Wade wrote back, assuring the woman that it's possible to exercise religious tolerance without pretending agreement, and that "thinking less" of someone's opinions doesn't mean thinking less of that person.

"There is what you think of a person's beliefs, and then there's how you treat that person. You can consider their beliefs to be ridiculous, yet you don't have to put an effort into openly ridiculing the person. You can lack respect for their beliefs, yet you can still treat the person respectfully."

He explained that the type of tolerance most people want to practice consists of three things, which he defined as follows:

> ***1. General respectful conduct.*** *Refraining from unnecessary, out-of-context, cruel or humiliating ridicule or derision of someone's religious beliefs.*
>
> ***2. Supporting civil rights.*** *Refraining from interfering with the free belief and practice of someone else's religion, as long as that practice does not violate civil law.*
>
> ***3. Discretion.*** *Knowing when to challenge a religious claim and when to disregard it; who to confront, and who to quietly abide; knowing when to call something a lie, when to call it ignorance, and whether or not either course is worth it; knowing how to balance principles, prudence and pragmatics in each case.*

There's that word again: *discretion*. Like respect, discretion is a learned behavior. One father who responded to my survey said he didn't see a problem with "ridiculing ridiculous ideas." I doubt that's true.

If the parent had a bit more time to reflect, I bet he would have found the problem: Parents who don't exercise discretion when talking to their children about religion in the privacy of their own homes tend to raise children who have difficulty exercising discretion when talking to everyone else out in the world.

This father may not see a problem with "ridiculing ridiculous ideas" at home, but I bet he would be highly uncomfortable if his private ridicule led his child to be mean in public.

RECOMMENDED READING
The Golden Rule

In this adorable book written by Ilene Cooper and illustrated by Gabi Swiatowska, a little boy sees a billboard with his Grandpa. The billboard says, "Do unto others as you would have them do unto you." What follows is a sweet discussion about the ethic of reciprocity, and why it's so important. Many parents may be surprised to learn that the ethic of reciprocity did not begin with Christianity. Jesus didn't invent the idea of treating others the way you want to be treated anymore than did Muhammad, who said: "The most righteous of men is the one who is glad that men should have what is pleasing to himself, and who dislikes for them what is for him disagreeable." No, the basis for the Golden Rule existed long before Christianity or Islam or Buddhism or Hinduism. It's older even than Confucius. In fact, no one is quite sure when the idea was first written, much less conceived—it's *that* old. All we know is that the general idea of the Golden Rule is as ubiquitous as it is beautiful, having existed in virtually every culture on Earth for many thousands of years.

Raising Kind, Compassionate Kids

Some parents, particularly non-believers, struggle with how to raise children whose tolerance of religion is not diminished by disbelief.

"My child is less tolerant of religious ideas that she thinks are 'stupid,' like creationism," said a West Virginia mother of one. "Letting her have her own opinion while teaching her not to be a jerk about it is somewhat difficult."

Tolerance does not mean having no strong convictions, or keeping those convictions to yourself. There is nothing at all wrong with criticizing people for saying hateful things or doing harmful things. You may discuss, oppose, even argue. But try to do it without name-calling or degradation—even when you see others name-calling and degrading you.

Here are some more tips for teaching tolerance in your secular home.

Watch your language. Stay clear of stereotypes, and suppress any and all generalizations in favor of specifics. For example, instead of saying, "Mormons do such and such," you might say, "Some Mormon people do such-and-such." Or, better yet, "Some people in that particular Mormon sect do such-and-such." Also, try to comment on actions, whenever possible, as opposed to belief. The right and wrong of actions are far more clear-cut than the beliefs that motivate them.

Cite your sources. Whether you're quoting something that a religious person said, or giving information about religion, give credit where credit is due. Pretend you're writing a news article, as opposed to an editorial.

Stay away from 'stupid' (and all its synonyms). Do not insult the intelligence of a person based solely on their religious beliefs. Religion is too much about feelings and emotions to be used as a sign of one's brainpower. People aren't stupid or gullible just because they believe certain things. And, by the way, you're not arrogant or cocky just because you don't.

Don't let logic overshadow kindness. Yes, non-believers often have science, logic, and rationality on their side. But thinking critically about other's beliefs is very different from criticizing others' beliefs. Explain to your child that people have lots of different reasons for believing the way they do and sometimes those reasons won't be logical or based in science. But everyone has a right to their own personal beliefs, and they don't deserve to be made fun of, or talked into changing those beliefs.

Humanize other points of view. Acknowledge and respect differences within your own circle of family members and friends, and make a point to reference them when talking about religion. If your son has a friend who is Jewish or an uncle who is atheist or a grandmother who is Christian, be sure to share that.

Make sure your children feel accepted and loved, no matter what. In *The Nature of Prejudice*, psychologist Gordon Allport writes that children are more likely to grow up tolerant if they live in a home that is supportive, and where children feel valued and respected.[18] So let's, you know, make that happen.

Stereotyping is a Two-Way Street

Non-believers may not be religion's biggest fans, but almost all have religious friends and family. Among those surveyed, for instance, 86 percent said they had religious family, and 93 percent said they had religious friends.

"My own close friends who are deeply religious get a free pass from me," said one. "They are not homophobic, but they are pro-life. I am pro-choice. We love each other and agree to not really discuss those areas where we don't agree."

"Religion is abhorrent," said another, "but my friends are quite nice!"

These double standards exist within all of us. But each of us would do better by our children if we tried harder to be fair and steer clear of stereotypes whenever possible. That goes for believers, too.

Here are some of the more common stereotypes we need to retire.

Non-Believers	**Believers**
They hate religion and religious people.	They want to convert everyone else to their point of view.
They raise their kids without a moral code.	They think everyone outside their faith will go to hell.
They are anti-Christmas.	They're uneducated, conservative, and closed-minded.
They are liberal, Fox News-bashing, tax-loving socialists.	They reject evolution and distrust science.
They are arrogant, angry, militant, selfish, and generally unpleasant to be around.	They think the Bible is factual and/or the word of God.
They worship the devil.	They support school prayer.
They secretly believe in God.	They would never elect an atheist president.
They turned away from religion because of a bad experience or trauma.	They are homophobic and sexist.
They are selfish, materialistic, and don't give to charity.	They love Fox News.
They can't be trusted.	They use religion as a "Get Out of Jail Free Card."
They enjoy trampling on people's rights to express their religious beliefs in public.	They use prayers in lieu of offering practical help.
They stereotype believers.	They stereotype non-believers.

FROM THE BLOG

Where's an Omniscient Police Officer When You Need One?

The other two members of my little family had another great God Talk recently. This one presented Charlie with a chance to discuss with Maxine a little about honesty, diversity, and the importance of kindness.

Maxine: Where do you think God is? Like, which house or school.

Charlie: I don't think God is anywhere. I don't believe there is such a thing as God.

Maxine: But if you did, where do you think he is?

Charlie: Well, people who believe in God believe he is everywhere and sees everything. They believe he is with everyone, watching over you.

Maxine: Is he with bad guys?

Charlie: They think he is everywhere.

Maxine: God is with bad guys?

Charlie: Yeah. They think God wants you to make good decisions, and even if you are making bad decisions, God is with you so when you are ready to do good things, he'll be there. They think God is there to help you and protect you. (Pause.) Other people who believe in God think he made the world and then kind of stepped back. He just watches from heaven to see what we'll do, but he doesn't interfere or help. Like the whole world is a big science experiment.

Maxine: A HUGE experiment.

Charlie: What do you believe?

Maxine: (Exasperated, like 'I've told you a hundred times') I believe in God on Wednesdays and Sundays.

Charlie: But what do you believe about God? Is he everywhere?

Maxine: I think he stepped back.

[Pause.]

Maxine: I believe in God on Sundays and Wednesdays because Sunday is the day for church, and Wednesday is so I can have a school day.

[Pause]

Maxine: Is God good or bad?

Charlie: Everyone who believes in God believes he is good.

Maxine: I wish the biggest policeman in the world climbed a huge giant ladder up to heaven and there was a huge microphone as big as five million houses stacked on top of each other and the policeman said into the microphone, 'God is real!' or 'God is not real!' and then everyone would know and everyone would believe the same thing.

Charlie: It's hard not knowing, isn't it?

Maxine: Yeah.

Charlie: [Pause] What I think is it doesn't really matter what you believe. What you think doesn't matter. It's what you *do* that matters.

Maxine: Or say.

Charlie: Right. You can think whatever you want. I can think someone is stupid . . .

Maxine: But don't say it to them. 'Hey, you're dumb!'

Charlie: Right. It's what you do and say that matter. Think whatever you want.

Maxine: Because we don't want to hurt their feelings.

Charlie: Right.

When it comes down to it, "tolerance" is just a way of asking people not to be total dicks to one another. Tolerance doesn't mean just barely holding back your hatred, nor does it require you to endure the hate of others or to treat religion with undeserved reverence, or to stand by while people do bad things for religious reasons. It also doesn't mean that you can't laugh or joke about religion, or watch Bill Maher anymore. Jokes are jokes; we all need to let off steam once in a while. And having a sense of humor about all things, religion included, is the smartest way I know to get through life.

At its core, tolerance just means being nice, being fair, being courteous—even when dealing with beliefs that you don't believe to be true. And, more than anything, it means looking at many aspects of a person, not just one aspect, before drawing conclusions about that person's character.

Yes, it's hard to be kind when confronted by people who are unkind (or just freaking dumb), or to be courteous to people showing no courtesy to you. But this is one place where it would help our kids—and the world—to try to become a model for the change we seek, and to teach our children to do the same.

CHAPTER SIX *Critical Thinking: Our Ace in the Hole*

These days critical thinking is an essential component of a safe childhood experience. We parents constantly advise our youngsters to resist peer pressure, to bring reasoning and analysis to their school studies, to question what they see on TV, and to be skeptical of what they encounter on the Internet. These lessons in discernment start early. When children are barely out of diapers, we start stressing the difference between "safe" strangers, like police officers, and strangers to be wary of, like everyone else.

Yet, despite this constant focus on critical thinking, millions of parents—Good parents! Nice parents!—offer their children no choice at all when it comes to religious beliefs. Instead, many children are taught to put their faith in one particular god, to trust that the Lord has a plan for them, that Muhammad paved a way for them, that Jesus will save them, that the saints will watch over them, and that a devil may tempt them to do "bad things" for which they could be eternally punished. That many religious parents do so with little concern as to how those messages may affect their children's ability to think critically is a testament to a gaping dichotomy of expectations they have for their youngsters. *Think for yourself*, these parents seem to be saying, *until it comes to religion*. Religion gets a pass.

In general, non-religious families have a less complicated view of critical thinking. Teaching kids to think critically does two things for us: It ensures that our kids have the skills necessary to make up their own minds; and it ensures that they do not buy into *any* ideas simply because people—or books or movies or advertisements—say they are true.

And, in that sense, for parents who wish for their children to accept nothing at face value, critical thinking truly is our ace in the hole.

Putting the 'Critical' in Critical Thinking

Children do an awful lot of thinking in school. They listen. They read. They study. They memorize. They acquire all kinds of knowledge, and then are tested on that knowledge.

But *critical* thinking is a little different. Critical thinking isn't the process of acquiring knowledge from others, but the process of analyzing knowledge for ourselves. Critical thinking involves questioning what others say, talking things out, looking at problems from a number of different angles, and coming up with good solutions.

Ideally, critical thinkers are open-minded and mindful of alternatives, curious and well-informed, good judges of credibility, able to identify reasons and assumptions, able to develop and defend a reasonable position regarding a belief or action, and cautious when drawing conclusions.

So how do we encourage these values and behaviors in our kids? What can we parents do to supplement the direction they may be receiving from schoolteachers?

When I asked this of a number of parenting experts, certain patterns arose almost immediately. Almost all of the experts I interviewed, for example, advised parents to include their children in the decision-making process. Letting kids watch us work through our problems shows them how to weigh factors and use common sense and logic before reaching conclusions.

Experts also encouraged parents to ask open-ended questions. Instead of trying to convince our kids that we are right, we should engage in dialogues that encourage them to think for themselves.

Laurie Gray, who runs a company called Socratic Parenting, pointed out that there are few better ways to do that than by reading together as often as possible. She said:

> *Regardless of what you read, when you read with your child, you can engage him in a meaningful dialogue. Don't just read for content. Enjoy the stories and explore the elements. The key is to ask open-ended questions and really listen to what your child says. Some helpful open-ended questions are "What did you like about?" or "What did you think about?" or "What else might [the character] have done?"*

What some people miss is that critical thinking is directly linked to self-esteem. Kids who don't have confidence in themselves are less likely to think they can solve their own problems. So part of raising a critical thinker is building up our children's confidence.

To that end, Samantha Madhosingh, a clinical psychologist and personal coach, contends that parents must teach their kids to do things for themselves as early and often as possible.

> *As parents we often want to do everything for our children, including making all their decisions for them and/or undermining any decisions they may make, she said. By doing this we diminish their sense of mastery and self-confidence. For young people to feel capable and develop critical-thinking skills they need practice at doing things and learning from their mistakes.*

Bill Corbett, the author of *Love, Limits, & Lessons: A Parent's Guide to Raising Cooperative Kids*, agreed. He suggested that, when our children come to us with a problem—such as boredom or peer pressure—we acknowledge the feelings we see in our kids and then ask them what they can do to solve it. "Offer to help," he said, "but do not fix it for them. If your child draws pictures with flaws (airplanes with wheels on the roof), avoid pointing them out, and relax."

Both Corbett and Gray emphasize the importance of active listening. When you ask a question, Gray said, "give your child time to answer." And whatever their answer, "respond with something that acknowledges rather than judges the answer as good or bad, right or wrong." React in a neutral way, she said, while also asking focused follow-up questions.

"This empowers kids to identify their own feelings, motives, and conflicts and begin to live with more self-awareness."

Letting Kids Challenge Us—and Win

It is a common misconception in the freethought movement that children learn to be skeptical by being told what to be skeptical about. In reality, children develop skepticism by being allowed to think independently and ask questions for themselves, not by being told who to question and what questions to ask.

The irony is that the best way to make sure our children are both able and willing to organize and formulate their own arguments is not by telling them what to challenge, but by letting them challenge *us*.

Linda Hatfield, parenting coach and co-founder of a Southern California-based parenting program called Parenting from the Heart, said the only way to truly empower children is to let them protest our decisions and opinions, take part in decision-making, and (a good amount of the time, at least) get their way.

Other common methods of working through problems—punishment, shame, guilt, bribery, and rewards—are self-esteem killers, she said. And parents who rely on these methods lose out on excellent opportunities to let kids think through problems for themselves. Hatfield insists that kids be able to challenge their parents without being punished for it.

"Even if you don't agree" with them, she said, "give them credit when they do their own thinking."

In this way, she said, children will learn that it's good to question what we tell them. And they'll respect our decisions and advice far more for the rest of their lives because we have respected them first.

"What I think is most important," Hatfield said, "is what we model."

Now, I'm the first to admit, this is easier said than done. Young children are just so damn *immature* sometimes. They never just say: "Gee, Mommy, I strongly disagree with you. Please reconsider your decision and let me have that ice cream now rather than making me wait until later." Instead, they scream and cry and spit and embarrass us in public places. It's tough. Even when we do think they have the right to challenge us, we often don't feel we can, in good conscience, give in to their demands because they've been such meanies about it. *I will not be yelled at*, we tell ourselves. *Respect is non-negotiable.*

But Hatfield, who runs her parenting courses and workshops alongside her husband, a retired police officer named Ty, asks parents to understand that most of what they consider *misbehavior* is actually age-appropriate behavior. Kids, she said, are behaving not to be "bad" (a word she loathes) or to show disrespect, but because they're going through normal developmental stages and don't have the skills yet to challenge you calmly and courteously.

By all means, she suggested, tell them that screaming (or whatever they're doing) is not okay. But then take a moment to allow yourself to reconsider your own conduct or decisions. Would it hurt you to let them win? Maybe it's a good time to say "yes" to the ice cream or the extra ten minutes of playtime. If nothing else, she said, encourage your kids to help find a compromise that works for both of you.

In short, instead of chastising them for challenging us, Hatfield asks parents to focus more on the message, not the method, and to stop taking things so dang personally.

Dale McGowan, co-author of *Raising Freethinkers: A Practical Guide to Parenting Beyond Belief*, among other secular parenting books, told me he talks about this in his workshops. He said:

> *My kids heard from a very early age that they always have the right to know the reason for a decision and to question it if they feel it's wrong or unfair. I told them I couldn't just say 'Because I said so,' and the few times I've said that, they've gleefully called me on it. I've made a point of changing my mind, out loud, when they have a good point. That does more for their growing autonomy than almost anything else I can do. I can attest that the result of all this is not chaos but a pretty smoothly functioning home with scads of mutual respect.*

It would be too simplistic to suggest that authoritarian parenting allows no room for skepticism. But the two things *are* related, and if we want to raise critical thinkers who naturally question what they hear from others, it would behoove us to stop feeling frustrated when kids challenge us—and start feeling proud.

FROM THE BLOG

Can the Bible Help Kids Think Critically?

Once upon a time, I would have choked on the idea of buying a children's Bible for my daughter. The way I saw it, the Bible was an indoctrination tool. I no more wanted to crack that book open than I wanted to get her baptized or plan her Bat Mitzvah or teach her to pray toward Mecca five times a day. It was all the same to me. In my mind, only believers read the Bible.

But times have changed.

Today, I don't equate the Bible with religion; I equate it with religious literacy. It is the quickest and most effective way to expose kids to Western belief systems. When it comes to knowledge of Judaism and Christianity and—to a slightly lesser extent—Islam, you can't do better than to read some key Bible passages. Judaism relies heavily on Moses and the book of Exodus. Christianity revolves around the Gospels: Matthew, Mark, Luke, and John. And a central force in Islam is Abraham of Genesis.

So, when Maxine was about five, I began reading her the Bible. Well, not the Bible, exactly, but rather a version of the Bible made for small children—with far more pictures than words.[19] Yes, the book oversimplified things. Yes, the stories were whitewashed. And gone was all the great language that makes the Bible at all enjoyable to read. But the greater good was that my kid understood the stories and was drawn into them enough to actually remember them.

Maxine has had her children's Bible for years now. Early on, she would take it out and look at the pictures, but by age eight, she was picking it up to read on car rides. She was most fascinated by the moral aspects of each tale.

All kids go through a periods where they think quite a lot about the line between "right" and "wrong." They become little police officers, reminding us of the rules and holding us to them. That's part of the reason Maxine was drawn to the stories in the Bible; they were larger-than-life tales, so the degrees of rightness and wrongness were heightened.

The shocking thing about it all is that—contrary to the common assumption—reading the Bible seemed to help hone her ability to think critically. She read the stories with genuine interest and serious consideration but without the reverence, deference, and praise associated with faith-based Bible classes. It was remarkable, really, especially when I think back on the pure lack of critical thinking I employed when I heard the same stories as a kid.

One day, for example, while reading in the car, she got to the tenth of the Ten Commandments and read (aloud): "Never want what belongs to others."

Then she stopped reading and took issue with Moses.

"Well, you can *want* what belongs to others," she said. "You just can't *have* it. You can buy one for yourself."

In the story about Joseph's dream coat, the passage read: "Joseph was one of Jacob's twelve sons. Jacob loved him more than all of his other sons."

Maxine looked up at me, "*That's so mean*!" she said.

When Joseph is thrown in jail, and one of the other prisoners asks Joseph—quite out of the blue —to decipher his dream, Maxine was all: "Well how would *he* know what that means?!" And when Abraham tells his son, Isaac, that he must marry whoever God chooses for him, Maxine declared that to be "dumb" and explained to me that, of course, Isaac can marry whoever he wants.

But my favorite bit was when her Bible told her that "goodly people" would go to live in heaven.

"I am a goodly person," Maxine said, "but I don't want to live in heaven."

And then she added: "Where do all the *badly* people go?"

Encouraging kids to hone their critical-thinking skills has a number of benefits, only one of which is their likelihood to question other people's opinions, beliefs, and actions later in life. Whether those "other people" are charismatic religious leaders or libidinous high school boyfriends, the value of that particular skill is obvious. But teaching our kids to think critically does require us to tame the control freaks within us all. It means watching, from the outside, as they make their way through this maze of life and trusting that they'll find their way back to us one way or another.

At times that may require small leaps of faith, if you will, but the results are well worth it.

CHAPTER SEVEN *Kickstarting Religious Literacy*

Several years ago, an atheist friend of mine agreed to send his eight-year-old son to a Vacation Bible School camp with some friends from the neighborhood. As camp week approached, the two would discuss "VBS" from time to time. One day, his son asked: "Dad, what does VBS stand for?"

"Vacation Bible School," my friend answered.

To which his son replied: "What's a Bible?"

It was a bit of a wake-up call for my friend—who, until then, hadn't wholly considered the value of educating his kid in the ways of religion at such an early age.

Most of the religious parents I've interviewed do understand the importance of religious literacy. In my survey, 95 percent of parents said they wanted their children to be educated in the ways of religion. Here are some of the reasons they named.

> *Teaching them about religious literature eliminates fear and hopefully helps to make the world a better place . . . by understanding those beliefs.*
>
> *It's important to understand, even if you don't believe.*
>
> *You can't get away from religion. It is part of the fabric of the human story.*
>
> *I want my children to make their own choices based on what they learn about different religions.*
>
> *Religion is a HUGE part of all cultures, and there are so many different philosophies involved. I want my children to understand the world, including spirituality.*
>
> *It is good to have an all-around education about most aspects of life.*

So that they might find a larger purpose and meaning to life.

You can't talk about why you don't believe in something if you aren't
educated about it somewhat to begin with.

Knowledge is power.

Despite these thoughtful answers, many parents went on to say that they didn't quite know what a religious education entailed, or how best to go about it.

"I believe in religious literacy," one mom told me candidly, "but I'm doing a terrible job at it."

But why? Why are so many secular parents dropping the ball when it comes to this stuff? Well, some lack the knowledge or interest in religion themselves. Others just can't seem to find a decent starting point. But the refrain I hear more than any other is that parents do try to talk about religion and that the kids don't want to hear it. They find it boring. As in: Boooooo-riiiiiing. And, as every parent knows, when a kid's bored with a conversation, the conversation is basically over.

Scoot Over, Dora: Making Room for Jesus, Muhammad, and Vishnu

To a certain extent, boredom can't be helped. Sometimes we have to tell our kids things they aren't interested in hearing. But in my experience, when it comes to religious literacy, an awful lot of boredom can be traced to poor timing.

In an effort to wait until kids are "old enough," we miss our window. Young children are just more dialed into us. They want to be around us; they want to hear what we have to say. Wait too long, and they've lost much of that genuine interest in us and have turned to their friends for meaningful conversation. Trying to force religious talks with older children can become awkward, unnerving, contrived, and difficult. Plus, we may feel rushed and rely on lectures to get us through, rather than looking for real-world opportunities to arise.

"But what if my young child isn't interested in religion?" you might ask. "Shouldn't I wait until he is?"

Well, that depends. Certainly we don't want to push information on our kids prematurely. But let's not use their silence as an excuse, either. Kids can't ask about things they've not been exposed to. They're not going to show interest in something you treat as uninteresting.

The goal is to incorporate some religious knowledge into your child's everyday life, to make it light and fun and interesting (not unlike the popular preschool TV heroine *Dora, the Explorer*), and to resist the overwhelming urge to get too serious about any of it.

Here's the thing: Some people who believe in God or Allah are serious about religion because they want their kids to avoid going to hell. People who don't believe in God or Allah are serious about it because they worry their kids will think religion is great and end up drinking the Kool-Aid. But both these positions are based in fear, and the result of all this seriousness is that religion becomes a total bore. Too few of us are fighting boredom by making religion fun or funny or surprising—you know, stuff kids like.

Our very first conversations have the potential to be quite lively: "Some people believe God is a magic being in the sky who made the entire world!" That is mind-blowingly cool-sounding stuff. But when we're preoccupied with whether our kids will believe it, we are far more likely to couch all religious talk in ways that make it seem almost somber.

Recently, I Googled "Making religion fun." Nine out of the ten sites that popped up first were not about "making religion fun" but about "making fun of religion." Society is on a kick right now, and a lot of non-believers are counteracting religious indoctrination by making light of those beliefs as often, and as publicly, as possible. But for parents who want their kids to be religiously literate, that may be shortsighted.

Take Adam and Eve in the Garden of Eden, for example. If you're too busy explaining to your child that Adam and Eve weren't really the first people and that those who believe such things are irrational, you're probably not telling the Adam and Eve story very well. And that's a shame! Because it's a really great story, as well as being a vital addition to our kids' cultural knowledge.

Categories of Literacy

Now, I know *literacy* is a heavy word, but please don't think of it like school. This is not about having some rigid curriculum in place. It's about coming up with creative, interesting ways to expose your kid to religion, and then doing it bit by bit over a long stretch of time. Remember, we're not looking to inundate your child with information she doesn't want.

Let's start with the basics. There are two main aspects to religious literacy: what you teach, and how you teach it. Goals and tactics. What follows are six avenues into religious literacy.

Core beliefs. These refer to a religion's main dogma—including philosophical ideas about how we came to be, the meaning and purpose of life, and what happens after we die.

Stories. These are legends (real or not) involving religious belief. Stories are usually about God or gods, about legendary figures and religious leaders. This type of literacy is the easiest for parents to teach and the easiest for children to grasp.

Customs. These are all the activities associated with religion. This type of literacy generally involves all five senses—seeing, hearing, touching, smelling, and tasting. People's styles of worship and dress are customs. So are their eating habits (kosher, halal), their rites of passage (baptisms, pilgrimages), and their holidays (Diwali, Eid-al-Adha).

History. This refers to historical facts about how religions began and evolved. The split between Catholics and Protestants during the Reformation is an example of religious history.

Current events. This refers to the ways in which religion plays into politics and world events. This includes religion's role in local, national, and international conflicts, as well as in political elections and governmental decisions.

That's a lot, isn't it? Just keep in mind, it's not your job to teach it all, and it's not your child's job to know it all.

Being literate in religion doesn't require having a PhD in religious studies. It simply requires some elemental knowledge of world religions. You might think of it in the same way one is *literate* in American geography. The average American doesn't know the capital of every state, the name of every mountain range, or the location of every river. But she probably recognizes the shapes of most of the states and knows their proximity to one another. She probably knows the general climate differences between each part of the country.

And she *definitely* knows the difference between Disneyland and the White House.

Likewise, to understand religion, your child need not know the names of all the Hindu gods, the year Buddhism was founded, or the names of all the books included in the Old and New Testaments. But she should probably know that Hindus believe in more than one god, that the Buddha was the man who started Buddhism, that the Old and the New Testaments are two different parts that make up the Christian Bible, and that the second part has all the stuff about Jesus.

Five Steps to a Literacy Plan

How do you kick things off? That's easy; just look around.

For a young child, there's no such thing as a routine trip. A mundane errand for you is the road to discovery for them. Any image can prompt a question. *Why is the sun so bright? What kind of dog is that? Why are those two holding hands? Why does that woman's dress go all the way over her head?* Through a religious lens, every question can be used to illuminate some aspect of religion. But to the secular eye, the only image that needs some religious explaining is the woman in the hijab.

People wearing traditional religious attire are wonderful conversation starters because they're not a concept, they're a person—often right in front of you. The same is true of religious buildings and symbols, or holiday decorations. They are tangible and visible, as opposed to conceptual and vague.

"That's a nativity scene," you might explain. "It's there to tell us a story."

Remember, keep it simple. A couple of sentences usually does it. The woman's dress that covers her head, for example, deserves a simple answer about religious practices. "Different religions have different rules. In Islam, many women cover themselves to show they are good Muslims. She's wearing a hijab."

"So that other lady doesn't believe in God?" the child might ask. "Who knows?" you can say. "Plenty of people have beliefs that don't involve what they wear."

If the child takes the thing at face value, let it go. No sense dwelling if the kid has moved on. The trick (if there is a trick to this) is to let the child's curiosity be your guide. Try not to tell her more than she wants to know, or answer questions she's not asking. There's no need for a dissertation. None of this needs to be forced or coerced. If talking about religion is anything other than natural and interesting, you're probably trying too hard.

Now, eventually, natural inquisition may begin to taper off. You may run out of conversation starters. And you may want to devise a more formalized plan. Don't feel you must. Again, each family is different. But if you're big into planning and think it will help, here's an outline for how to go about it.

1. Set your goals.

Forget what other people think your kid should know. What do you think your kid should know? Would you like him to know the names of the religions and roughly what each represent? Do you want your child to be able to identify various deities and religious leaders? Or to be familiar with the major sacred texts? Maybe you would be satisfied if your child understood religious references, symbols, and the customs of your community. In his widely read book, *Religious Literacy: What Every American Needs to Know—And Doesn't*, author Stephen Prothero suggests tailoring literacy plans to the areas in which you live.[20] For instance, New Mexico and Arizona residents might want to know more about Native American folk religions; those in Miami should learn a bit about Santeria; Californians would do well to study up on Sikhism, and so on. Or maybe you'd simply like your child to understand generally what each religion believes, why they believe it, and why you don't. Whatever the case, list your essentials on a piece of paper—the things you want your kid to find out before he enters college. Discuss the list with your partner, if applicable, being sure to edit and revise as the two of you see fit. These are your goals.

2. Consider your child's interests.

Think about all the things that you and your child enjoy doing together. Do you take walks, listen to music, read books? Do you enjoy taking trips? Cooking together? Making or building things? Telling stories? Throwing parties? Do you have movie nights? Write it all down—and try to be as specific as possible.

3. Consider your child's temperament.

Is your child easily distracted? Is he adaptable? Is he sensitive to scary things? Social? Shy? Intense? Is he always on the move, or does he prefer to sit quietly and read? Does he value organization and routine, or appreciate spontaneity? And what kind of learner does he seem to be? Is he auditory (likes to talk things out), visual (prefers to see things) or hands-on (learns best by doing)? Write that down, too.

4. Brainstorm.

Now that you have a handle on your child's uniqueness, start brainstorming ways to slip your religious literacy goals into his life. Keep in mind that short spurts usually work best—a book here, a word definition there. Try to think of ways you can add a little literacy into what you and your child do together already. Challenge yourself to make it as playful as possible—so playful that your child doesn't know he's learning.

Here are some examples.

- **Books and Stories.** This is, bar none, the easiest way to get religious literacy into your life. Go to the library and dig up as many interesting-looking books as you can. The more pictures, the better. And don't forget to talk about the stories afterward as you would any other piece of literature—what did your child take away from the story? What did she like? What didn't she? (Read on for tips on choosing books appropriate for secular families and for specific book recommendations.)

- **Celebrating *All* the Holidays.** Put major religious holidays (such as the Jewish holiday of Rosh Hashanah, the Hindu holiday of Diwali, the Christian holiday of Easter, and the Muslim holiday of Eid al-Adha) on your calendar, and use them as opportunities to talk about various traditions. Don't worry if you don't know what the hell they are; you can Google them when the time comes. Make some traditional decorations; bake a food associated with that holiday; choose one activity to participate in; and tell the story of that holiday—being sure to give it a context within the religion. Then do it all again next year. (And please be sure to see the appendix for some examples of how to celebrate these and other holidays in a secular way!)

- **Toys and Games.** There are all kinds of religiously themed toys online: plush Confucius dolls, Jesus action figures, Barbies wearing Hindu saris. My favorite is the Create Your Own Deity magnet set, which can be found at *www.philosophersguild.com* (Flying Spaghetti Monster included). My daughter loves mixing and matching parts of different gods on the side of the refrigerator.

Whatever the case, be sure not to make a big deal out of the toys. No reason Confucius can't hold court with Winnie-the-Pooh and his friends. And Hindu Barbie is just another ridiculously proportioned plastic doll to add to the cadre of others. At the end of the day, if your child learns the words "Hindu" and "sari," that's a win.

• **Field Trip.** When given the opportunity, visit a temple, synagogue, church, mosque, or other place of worship. Call ahead if you're unsure of visiting hours or rules. And look for cultural events in your community that you can tie into religious customs—the Day of the Dead, for instance, or the Chinese New Year.

• **Movie Night.** Check out Netflix for movies that might be fun to watch. Just be sure they're age-appropriate. That is to say: Hold off on *Jesus Camp* until the kids are older, yeah? And no *VeggieTales*, please.

• **Museum Scavenger Hunt.** If you're going to a museum with religious art, make it a game for your child to find certain items in the art, including religious symbols. Write (or draw) things you want her to find: a chair, a book, a halo, an angel, etc. Then offer her a small monetary reward for every symbol she finds to spend in the museum gift shop afterward. (Check online first to get a sense of the art.) This is also a great way to ensure you get to see more than one room of the museum!

• **A Little Help From Your Friends.** Mix things up by encouraging friends and family with different beliefs to tell your kid a bit about them, or better yet, ask them to invite you to their next holiday celebration. (My daughter had a great time joining her friend's Passover dinner one year.)

• **Rock Out.** Download songs from each religion to make an all-religions playlist to listen to in the car. They could be children's songs, gospel songs, hymns, traditional chants—you name it. The only requirement is that you present a range of music highlighting more than one faith (and that you include Tim Minchin's *White Wine in the Sun* on your playlist). Then sit back and enjoy the questions that the music will generate!

- **Get Crafty.** Making crafts with a religious bent might help hold your child's attention for long enough to get in some literacy. I'm not advocating that you chisel little wooden crosses or anything, but making a collage with symbols of various belief systems could be fun. I recently made an all-religions charm bracelet for Maxine using all the religious symbols I could find in my local bead store. Now she has a fun (and jangly) way to familiarize herself with various religious symbols.

- **The Columnist's Trick.** I have a friend who is a newspaper columnist, and every experience that guy has in his life seems to end up in a column. No matter how mundane the experiences were at the time (and believe me, some were very mundane), he manages to make them interesting in the retelling. It's as though his brain finds ways to make his life experiences seem fun and relevant. We can all take a page from this guy's book. Learn something new about religion—the definition of *holy*, say, or the Five Pillars of Islam—and your mind will find an interesting way to get that bit of knowledge into a normal, everyday conversation with your kid.

- **A Part of the Décor.** Is your kid a visual learner? Go for graphics and pictures. For example, print out pictures of famous religious leaders, as well as scientists and philosophers, and make a poster out of them for your child. Let a wall in your house serve as temporary headquarters for religious literacy.

- **Religion Fridays.** Why do you have to do all the work? Let your kids teach you a thing or two. Ask each member of the family to learn something about religion. Then, at dinner, share what you've learned.

5. Follow up.

Check in with yourself periodically. Is your plan working out like you expected? Does your child seem to enjoy your talks? Is he learning the words and concepts you had hoped he would? Why or why not? What could you improve upon? How could you tweak your plan to ensure you get back on track?

Choosing Religious Books Appropriate for Secular Families

As you can imagine, kids' religious titles run the gamut. Many focus on religious holidays; others contain more overarching material—stories about Sikhism or Native American beliefs or the parables of Jesus. Because a good number are written for religious children, not all of them are good matches for secular families. The worst of the bunch are indoctrination materials. But the best are quite good. They offer fun stories, interesting settings and clever text, and they do it so well that they don't feel like "learning experiences"—even though that's what they are. Here are some tips for choosing religious books appropriate for secular families.

Choose a book that will appeal to your kid. You know your kid and her taste more than anyone else. You know when a book (or toy or game) has a good chance of holding her interest, or no chance at all. If your nine-year-old is too old for an Easter story about a little lamb, put it back. If your child is only interested in princesses, maybe choose a book about the Jewish Princess Esther over a book about the Hindu God Shiva. Religious literacy isn't about jamming knowledge down kids' throats; it's about trying to appeal to your kids' natural interests.

Be sure it's age-appropriate. Before you buy a book, or check it out from the library and hand it on to your little one, give it a read. Lots of religious stories depict people—not to mention God—doing some pretty gnarly things. (The story of Noah's Ark is not nearly so charming when you consider that God exterminated every living creature on Earth except the few who got onboard.) If you find that a story needs to be heavily edited to share it, maybe it's not time to share that particular story. That said, if you find yourself sharing a cleaned-up Bible story with your child, no sweat. Just explain that there's a bit more to the story than that, but that this is fine for now.

Make it relevant. Read Ramadan stories during the month of Ramadan, and Good Friday stories around Easter. Try to introduce each book with a sentence about why you're reading it. As a side note, many books are secondary materials—books that are great to read *after* your kid has been introduced to certain concepts. *Hoppy Passover* by Linda Glaser, for instance, is a sweet book about a bunny family that holds a Seder; but because it assumes a basic understanding of Passover, it might be better as an accompaniment to another book, rather than standing on its own.

Check for historical accuracy. Accuracy is a biggie. As secular parents, the point of reading religious books is to teach our kids about religion. When authors manipulate religious history to the point the stories are no longer remotely accurate—and some do—the value for us is gone. Religious people might believe that their kids will get the correct story eventually, and may not be worried about these deviations. (Heck, they might even prefer revisionist history from time to time—especially when the revision creates a more believable, desirable, or compelling story.) But secularists are looking for the truth. And, just as often, the inaccuracies insult both believers and non-believers.

Be aware of slants and bias. Although it may surprise you, this is not necessarily a deal-breaker for me. Even books written from a religious perspective can be really well done and educational. It all depends on the nature and degree of the slant. With some titles, the only slant is the point of view. An author might use "we," for instance, instead of "they" when talking about the religious group featured in the book. But as long as you are comfortable addressing these slants as they pop up—"The author uses 'we' in this story because he, himself, is Jewish," for example—then this shouldn't be a problem. Some books, though, are intended to indoctrinate, and secular parents would do right to leave those behind. Sermonizing books will do nothing but confuse your child and annoy you.

Many religious storybooks are perfectly appropriate for secular families. Here are some of my favorites.

- *Amma, Tell me About Diwali!* (2011), *Amma, Tell Me About Holi!* (2011) and *Amma, Tell Me About Krishna!* (2012) by Bhatki Mathur

- *The Best Eid Ever* by Asma Mobin-Uddin and Laura Jacobsen (2007)

- *Between Earth and Sky: Legends of Native American Sacred Places* by Joseph Bruchac and Thomas Locker (1999)

- *Bubbe's Belated Bat Mitzvah* by Isabel Pinson (2014)

- *Buddha* by Susan L. Roth (2012)

- *Celebrate: A Book of Jewish Holidays* by Judy Gross and Bari Weissman (2005)

- *David and Goliath* by Beatrice Schenk de Regniers and Scott Cameron (1996)
- *DK Children's Illustrated Bible* by Selina Hastings and Eric Thomas (2005)
- *The Easter Story* by Brian Wildsmith (2000)
- *Exodus* by Brian Wildsmith (1998)
- *Guru Nanak: The First Skih Guru* by Rina Signh and Andree Pouliot (2011)
- *How Ganesh Got His Elephant Head* by Harish Johari and Vatsala Sperling (2003)
- *Joseph* by Brian Wildsmith (1997)
- *The Legend of Lao Tzu and the Tao Te Ching* by Lao Tzu and Demi (2007)
- *The Little Book of Hindu Deities: From the Goddess of Wealth to the Sacred Cow* by Sanjay Patel (2006)
- *Meet Jesus: The Life and Lessons of a Beloved Teacher* by Lynn Tuttle Gunney and Jane Conteh-Morgan (2008)
- *Muhammad* by Demi (2003)
- *Night of the Moon: A Muslim Holiday Story* by Hena Khan and Julie Paschkis (2008)
- *Noah's Ark* by Jerry Pinkney (2002)
- *Passover* by Miriam Nerlove (1989)
- *Rumi: Whirling Dervish* by Demi (2013)
- *The Three Questions* (2003), *Zen Shorts* (2005), and *Zen Ties* (2008) by Jon J. Muth

FROM THE BLOG
Honk If You Love Jesus

Driving Maxine home from school one day, I spotted a small group of teenage girls at a busy intersection a few blocks from our house. They were on the sidewalk, smiling and chatting and dancing along to nonexistent music. A few of them shook pom-poms. Two of them held up big, hand-painted signs that said: HONK IF YOU ♥ JESUS.

I live in a diverse, metropolitan area, so despite the girls' bright smiles and youthful enthusiasm, only one person appeared to be at all interested. The driver of a mini-van made a left turn in front of us, honking all the way through the intersection. A passenger then rolled down her window, leaned out, and gave the girls a solid whoop-whoop for their efforts. The girls hooted and hollered and whoop-whooped right back, their bodies gyrating with giddiness. United in Christ.

"Why did that car honk?" Maxine asked as we pulled away.

"They honked at those girls with the signs," I said.

"What did the signs say?" she asked.

"Honk if you love Jesus."

[Long pause.]

"But you didn't honk," she observed.

"No, I didn't."

"You don't like Jesus?" she asked.

"No," I said, "that's not it."

[Pause.]

"You don't *love* Jesus?" she asked.

She was really thinking this one through. And who could blame her? This was pretty confusing for a kid whose mind tends to be pretty literal.

"No, that's not it, either," I said.

The fact is, in a way, I *do* love Jesus. Maybe not the way I love a family member or friend, but the way I love celebrities whose work I respect and admire. I love Jesus the same way I love Franz Kafka and Steven Hawking. The way I love Joan Didion, Sarah Silverman, Ralph Fiennes.

(Okay, not exactly the way I love Ralph Fiennes.)

The point is, love is not just love when it comes to the love of Jesus. Just like belief is not just belief. In a literal sense, I do believe in Jesus. I believe he lived, and I believe he died. And I believe he was probably a really good and smart person who sought to be a model of how to lead a moral life—and to help his people live better, happier, more hopeful lives.

But, of course, that's not enough.

For me to honk my horn at those girls—and to support them in their endeavor to spread their religion on the street corner—I needed to not just love the idea of Jesus the man, but I needed to love the reality of Jesus the son of God. In order to whoop-whoop, I needed to believe not only that Jesus was a great man, but also that he was magical. And I needed to support them in their happy-go-lucky brand of proselytizing.

The girls' signs didn't come with disclaimers, but they should have.

So, there I was, in the car, defending my silence to an inquisitive kid.

"I actually do love Jesus," I ended up telling Maxine. "I think he was a fantastic person, and I think he tried really hard to make the world a better place. It's just that some people, Christian people, think he was the son of God, and that's why those girls were holding those signs. I don't believe he was the son of God, so I didn't honk. Does that make sense?"

"Yep," she said.

And that was that.

[Phew.]

Hopefully things go as smoothly for you when your child sees his first "Honk" sign.

Religious literacy, like cultural literacy in general, has so many benefits. It allows kids to understand the world's art, architecture, literature, and history—not to mention the endless supply of religious idioms and clichés they are bound to hear throughout their lives. It helps kids survive and thrive in a world of religious diversity, empathize with a full range of people, understand why blind obedience can be so dangerous, and recognize religious intolerance when they see it. It equips them to discuss current events, contradict misinformation, and debate or dismiss religious zealots. And it assists them as they arrive at their own opinions about faith.

But religious knowledge, like religious tolerance, doesn't just happen. We parents have to make it happen. Unfortunately, saying the word "Hanukkah" once a year and pointing out burkas in the airport just doesn't cut it. Knowledge requires context. Tolerance requires action. If we want our children to be interested in and respectful of those around them, we must knit a sense of interest and respect into our childrearing—today and throughout the year.

Remember, imparting religious knowledge to your child should not wear you out, or overwhelm you. Whether your kid becomes interested in religion as a field of study will be decided when he's much older. Your job is not to show him precisely how to assemble this enormous puzzle that is *Religion*, but, rather, to show him the picture on the box. Help him assemble some edge pieces.

He'll take it from there.

CHAPER EIGHT *Got Religious Baggage?*

We view religion through the imperfect prism of our experience: the teachings of parents, chit chat of friends; opinions of scholars and scientists; the beliefs of community, country, and world. All of this defines our perceptions of spirituality.

Religion is so popular and yet so flawed. It can lead to charity, love, and art just as easily as it can lead to violence, hate, and fear. Which version of religion we choose to see depends entirely on what version of events we want to emphasize. Those of us who have rejected religion tend toward the bleaker version.

"I am quite disgusted by religion at large," a Michigan mother of two told me. "I look at the Church's influence in Africa and how it condemns condom use while AIDS continues to destroy a generation of people. I look at the Religious Right's influence on American politics and how it affects my health as a woman. So much that is wrong with the world can be traced back to religion."

Of the non-religious parents surveyed for this book, 57 percent said they viewed religion "negatively, with exceptions." And when asked for specifics, they unleashed a tidal wave of unfavorable descriptions. These parents framed religion as insular and exclusive, hateful, hurtful, and outdated. They complained of religion's hypocrisy, deception, arrogance, bigotry, and intolerance. They said they thought religion created small-mindedness, fostered prejudice, provided false hope, demanded conformity, and blocked scientific progress. They called religion a waste of time and money, a hindrance to critical thinking, and generally detrimental to society.

Said a mother living in small town in Idaho: "I view organized religion negatively because I see it as a way for people to be manipulated and controlled, financially and emotionally, and a way to form and justify a 'mob mentality' that includes hate or harmful thoughts towards others—such as gays [and] people of other religions."

An Oregon father of two added: "The biggest problem is that religions teach their followers to disregard reason and to embrace nonsensical dogmatic thinking."

These are some harsh and undiluted observations, for sure. But they aren't inaccurate.

Religion *has* been used to manipulate and control. It *has* been used to justify hurtful and hateful thoughts toward others. It *has* been used to hinder critical thinking. The problem isn't that these statements are harsh or that these statements are false. The problem is that these statements are generalizations. They are true of some—maybe even many—but they are not true of all.

What's more, these same descriptions can be applied to any number of isms: nationalism, patriotism, and communism, not to mention partisan politics.

When Religion's Dark Side Looms Large

Author Cliff Edwards, who was raised a Christian, said his childhood faith experiences—which included threats of hell and feelings of shame and guilt—led to a lifelong struggle with personal resentment. In Edwards' book *The Forgiveness Handbook: A Simple Guide to Freedom of the Mind and Heart*, he calls his experiences "spiritual baggage," a play on the expression "emotional baggage," which refers to unresolved issues that tend to load people down.

Edwards said the book was, as you would imagine, sparked by his own experience. He said his baggage came in the form of "automatic judgments about people who held similar religious beliefs as those I was raised with, and an eagerness to make them wrong."

Take a minute to think about how you view religion in general. Do you think you may be carrying around some spiritual baggage yourself? Maybe you were told as a young child that you were a sinner or unclean; maybe you were made to feel guilty about certain thoughts or behaviors; maybe you were threatened with divine consequences that truly scared you; maybe you felt lied to or betrayed by religious authorities at some point. Or maybe your baggage is not personal; you are simply disturbed by the role religion plays in the world—how it has led to the discrimination against minorities and women, the abuse of children, the deaths of millions of people throughout history. Perhaps you are wildly empathetic to those whose lives and dreams have been limited, hampered, or destroyed by irrational beliefs.

If you're not sure whether your experiences have left you with a strong bias against religion, try answering these questions, posed by Edwards on his website, *Forgiving the Church:*

- *Do you feel limited or (personally) affected by outdated religious beliefs, values, or patterns of action?*

- *Are you annoyed or resentful about the morals or ethics you were taught as a child?*

- *Do you feel righteously indignant or blaming toward any religions, denominations, or religious leaders?*

- *Are you reluctant to share your spiritual beliefs with family or others who believe differently?*

- *Are you fearful or anxious about possible retribution from God for "sinful" thoughts or behaviors?*

- *Do you feel guilty or shameful about your wants, needs, or deeply held desires?*

The first step to subduing your faith-related resentment is acknowledging you have it. The second is to find a way to pack those negative feelings into a sturdier suitcase—one that's not spring-loaded, for instance, and likely to explode the moment your child touches it.

The Inheritance of Anxiety

To be clear, I'm not suggesting that you rid yourself of your bad feelings or try to resolve all your bitterness around religion. (That's another book entirely!) Your feelings about religion are yours, and you are entitled to them.

What I'm talking about is stopping short of passing on your frustration, anxiety, or bitterness to children who have no reason to be frustrated, anxious, or bitter and no firm grasp as to why they might feel that way.

Consider the following two stories shared with me by a pair of secular mothers who didn't think they were unloading their spiritual baggage on their children, and both of whom did just that.

First was the mother who told me that her young daughter once stormed out of her elementary school classroom, accusing the teacher of "indoctrinating" the class by telling them the Christian Easter story.

"I was very proud," the mother went on to say, that "my child was so confident, assertive, and sure of her own non-belief that she was able to do this."

Confident and assertive, yes. But sure of her own non-belief? In elementary school? That's doubtful. Most likely, the child was simply repeating a myth she'd picked up on at home: that talking about religious stories is a form of indoctrination.

Of course, there certainly is cause for concern when it comes to religion in public schools, especially if the only religious stories being shared are slanted toward one particular religion. But taken as an isolated incident, I am hard-pressed to understand the purpose of enlisting this young child in a battle she can't fully comprehend. By treating all religious beliefs as something dangerous, parents create openings for extreme views and overly emotional reactions. Which brings me to my second example. This one involves a mother whose childhood in a strict Roman Catholic family left her emotionally scarred. As an adult, she spoke of her religious views pretty openly in her home, not realizing her strong opinions were getting filtered down to her children—all under the age of eight. The results were mortifying.

"My son," she told me, "has expressed his hatred of religion in front of religious family members."

Hatred, people, and the kid wasn't yet nine.

It concerns me when I see parents raising their children, either accidentally or on purpose, to view religion—particularly Christianity—as a personal threat. First of all, most religious people are really nice. (*Your* friends are, right?) And those religious groups that *do* threaten civil liberties or support sexism or racism or homophobia or tribalism or all those other nasty things are not the sort your child is likely to join anyway. Why? Because you are raising them to be self-confident critical thinkers with a strong moral base and a genuine understanding of religious ideas.

You didn't skim over that sentence, did you? I'll repeat it once more just in case: As long as you are raising your kids to be *self-confident critical thinkers* with a *strong moral base* and a *genuine understanding of religious ideas*, your kid is very unlikely to accept any closed-minded religious dogma as true. Self-confidence will help prevent your kid from feeling compelled to believe something just because others do. Critical-thinking skills will help prevent your kid from adopting religious views without holding them under the microscope of their own skepticism. A moral base will help your kid avoid any organization (religious or otherwise) that contributes to the emotional or physical abuse of other people. And an understanding of religious ideas will help your kids refute misinformation and see through the claims of smooth-talking evangelists.

Plus, as I mentioned earlier, the fact that you have respected and trusted your child to adopt his own religious identity will set his personal status quo. Later in life, he is more likely to expect and insist that others respect his choices and decisions the way you have done for him.

'How Could Anyone Believe that Crazy Stuff?'

Let's face it, religion involves some pretty kooky ideas: Evil spirits taking control of pigs. Talking donkeys. The refusal of blood transfusions. Sacred underwear. Bread turning into human flesh. Water turning into wine. Supernatural beings revealing themselves in grilled cheese sandwiches. Alien spirits inhabiting our bodies. Virgin births. Sprinkling infants with special water to keep them out of hell. Refraining from masturbation because it's against God's wishes. Gathering in Jackson County, Missouri, just before the end of the world. Girls being submissive to boys. Waving a chicken over your head to take away your sins.

I could go on and on. We all could.

When kooky religious ideas come up—*and they will come up*—it may seem next to impossible to speak about them to kids without making some pretty harsh personal judgments, or to react without exasperation, incredulity or disparagement. So switch gears. Instead of focusing on the "truth" of bizarre claims, try to show some empathy for the believers. Focus on why people might believe things that sound pretty goofy to our ears.

To the question, "How could anyone believe that crazy stuff?" here are some potential answers.

Upbringing. "Sometimes people believe things because that's what they were taught to believe as children. If all your life you were told that there were a bunch of gods watching over you, or that Jesus walked on water, you might not ever question it. In fact, you might not like it that other people question it. In your mind, that's the truth and it might make you feel uneasy or confused or left out or even scared when people say otherwise."

Comfort. "People believe things because it makes them feel good. Heaven is a great example; it comforts people to believe that they, and the people they love, will go to heaven after they die. Also, some people believe they can talk directly with God, and they enjoy that feeling. Also, religion can make people feel less alone and more in control. When a person's life is bad, religion can help them have hope for the future."

Rules. "Rules don't seem that fun to kids, but they are really important. And some people need rules more than others. Religion provides rules for how to be a good person. It's like one big to-do list that was written a long, long time ago. Some of the rules might not make much sense in today's world, but because they are part of the old list, people do them anyway."

Feelings. "Some people believe things because they feel, deep down, that they are true. Something inside them tells them to have faith. We all have gut instincts—reasons we can't explain that make us feel a certain way about something—and the same is true of religious people. Sometimes their gut instincts tell them to believe."

Friends. "Religions are really good at bringing people together. Most of them have a building people can go to at least once a week and share their beliefs. People sit with each other and talk and laugh and make each other feel happy and valuable. It's like a second family. And when you love people, you want to agree with them. And when the people you love believe certain things, it can lead you to believe them, too. In other words, people often believe things out of a need for friendship and community."

Message in a Bottle

Some parents will have a harder time than others skating through these talks without going to religion's dark places, especially if they've been badly hurt by religion. Find yourself wanting to say things to your child that you probably shouldn't? Put it in a letter and seal it up. When your child is eighteen, you can give him the letter with a note about how hard it was sometimes to keep yourself in check. The fun part is that the letter will act as a time capsule for your beliefs. You may find that they've changed by then and be happier than ever that you decided not to make a big deal out of your beliefs in the first place. In the meantime, if something slips out that you regret, don't be afraid to show your cards. "It's hard for me to talk about this subject sometimes," you might tell your child, "because I've had some difficult experiences, but I'm doing the best I can. And it's really important to me that you decide what's right for you."

The Good Kind of Baggage

In the Netherlands, it's traditional to separate children by religion; schools often cater to one religion or another. But in 2010, a Dutchman named Aart Wouters bucked the trend when he founded The Kaleidoscoop School, which offers an "open and non-dogmatic environment" devoted to teaching children about all religions and worldviews—including atheism and agnosticism. The school's mission is to allow children the ability to make decisions for themselves about religion by giving them *bagage*—the Dutch word for baggage. Ironically, though, the Dutch version of baggage doesn't refer to negative judgments; it refers to knowledge or wisdom.

"Many adults," Wouters has said, "worry that children are not mature enough or their minds are not developed enough to handle multiple explanations of God, the universe, and creation. They fear children are not able to properly understand religion, and therefore learning about the variety of religions will just 'confuse' them rather than lead to true understanding and tolerance."[21] In truth, however, Wouters noted, it's the parents who have problems understanding and accepting multiple religious views—not the children.

I share Wouters' desire to speak about religion in more neutral terms, to turn down the volume on religious (or non-religious) proselytizing, and to make a concerted effort to raise compassionate human beings.

Again, it's okay to have negative opinions about religion. In our roles as individuals, we can be as negative as we like.

But, as parents, let's be sure that when we pass on our baggage to our kids, it's the Dutch variety—based on wisdom, not emotion.

FROM THE BLOG

Glenn Beck Conservatives Expose 'Notorious Atheist'

Back in 2010, I wrote a few books for the Girl Scouts. Somewhere in the editing process, someone added the name of *Media Matters*, a website that fact-checks "conservative misinformation," as a media-literacy resource for middle school Girl Scouts.

After the book was published, a mom reported the reference to a Glenn Beck-run website, after which a minor shit storm broke out. Fox News featured the issue on several segments, and a bevy of Internet commenters had a field day, especially after they'd discovered my blog for secular parents—which I started two years after writing the Girl Scouts books. Among other pleasantries, I was called "a notorious atheist who infiltrated the Girl Scouts" and likened to a serial killer ("Notice the three names," one guy wrote.)

But the Girl Scouts, as an organization, got it worse. They were accused of being a propaganda machine trying to indoctrinate young girls into liberalism, and opponents demanded the books be removed from bookshop shelves.

The insecurity being masked by all that seething anger was hard to miss. These conservatives were up in arms because of *one* link in *one* book. Said my husband of the dust-up: "If conservative values are so frail that they can be completely undermined by exposure to a single, slightly progressive website, those conservative values can't be very strong."

See why I married that guy?

The saddest part was that, despite the amazing opportunities and self-esteem girls receive from the Girl Scouts, many uber-conservative parents threatened to pull out their children en masse. And why exactly?

Because they were afraid their kids might see the name of a website? Because they thought they might actually click on the website and see what it had to say? Oh no! Crash! Bam! Boom! They saw! They saw! Now they're ruined!

Listen, conservative parents are not the only ones who are guilty of running away and hiding their kids from things they don't agree with. Liberals do it all the time. So do religious parents. So do non-religious parents.

Sheltering our kids from political and religious views that scare us is universal. And, yet, it's so much of what I'd like to see us move away from. Because if we parents really believe in the strength of our values and beliefs, then we ought to be confident that they'll compete well in the marketplace of ideas. We ought to be comfortable enough to let our kids see the world as it really is, and people as they really are.

The point here is not to get you to ignore religion's shortcomings—or allow abuses and bigotry to continue unchecked. But try to give those shortcomings the same weight as humanity's shortcomings. Even John Lennon, who asked the world to "imagine no religion" in his 1971 peace anthem "Imagine," also asked the world to imagine no country, no possessions, no greed, and no hunger. He never singled out religion as the only source of distress in the world. Just be careful not to give your kids the wrong impression.

Most of the people your kids will meet during their lifetimes will have something wonderful to offer the world, regardless of their beliefs. So if you do choose to speak of religion in negative terms, be sure to explain exactly what you oppose, and why. Let your children know that there are all sorts of reasons people have faith and all sorts of different types of believers in the world. Many of them experience the same feelings—love, joy, fear, sadness—as your kids do; they encounter the same challenges and opportunities; they have many of the same interests outside religion. Each religious person, like each non-religious person, brings something unique to the world.

Again, our job is not to convince our kids we're right; they're already inclined to think we're right. Instead, we must expose them to as many different ideas, beliefs, and ways of life as we can while we're still around to offer guidance.

Trust me, they can handle it. And, you know what? We can, too.

CHAPTER NINE *Celebrating Secularism, Science, and Sleeping in on Sundays*

This book has so far focused almost exclusively on the challenges of being a non-religious parent. But you know as well as I do: There is far more to celebrate than to lament.

Time and again, I find myself breathing a sigh of relief that I don't have to face the inevitable complications presented by religious ideas or adhere to ancient doctrine when making decisions about how best to raise my child. Mine is such a clear-cut worldview—logical and beautiful in its simplicity—and I am immensely proud to be a sharing it with my daughter.

Once, on my website, I asked parents to weigh in on the best part of being a secular parent. I got so many wonderful answers:

> *I would say that the single best thing is to teach children to think for themselves—question everything, no topic is off limit—make your own choices and be responsible for them.*

> *Knowing that my kid is ethical and makes good choices because that's who he chooses to be, not because he thinks someone is watching over his shoulder to punish him if he trips up.*

> *Not having someone else tell me what to think. Like the time my stepdaughter told me that Catholics are now allowed to 'believe in evolution.'*

> *I like being able to tell my kids answers to their questions that are logical and that make sense. Kids are natural scientists, wanting to know how the world works. Scientists need scientific answers!*

> *The amazing conversations I have with my daughter about spirituality, and the fact that she embraces it all with curiosity and without prejudice.*

> *Watching her develop an independent, internal moral compass.*

Living my own secular faith honestly.

Being able to be totally open about sexuality (when the age/ time is right).

Their thoughts are private and not sinful. No superstitions.

The way your life goes isn't all 'God's plan.'

You have very little invested in being right or wrong.

Being able to answer with 'I don't know.'

Teaching my kids to appreciate themselves and what they accomplish. So many religious people are too quick to thank their god for their successes. I want my kids to pat themselves on the back when they accomplish something.

I can stimulate and feed his curiosity and imagination, and allow him to think freely and form his own opinions and ideas about the world.

Being able to watch my son grow and learn without the fear of god/evil/heaven/hell in his decisions. He's a little kid, and he gets to live like one. He doesn't have a huge myth scaring him or guilting him into behaving a certain way (or 'else').

Teaching my kids that life is valuable because it's the only one we have.

Sleeping in on Sundays.

Feeding Our Secular Souls

All of this trumpeting of secularism is not meant to disparage religion, but to offer some balance and much-needed perspective. Just ask Alain de Botton.

If you've not heard of him already, de Botton is a British philosopher and author who penned the 2013 book *Religion for Atheists: A Non-believers Guide to the Uses of Religion*. In it, he makes a strong case for how atheists can borrow from religion's long history to connect with other non-believers, and to deepen our reverence for life in general.[22] Indeed, his book is a prescription for bringing rich meaning and purpose to the secular life. He famously created the first atheist church, an idea that is spreading throughout the United States as we speak. Whether you believe that such a church setting is necessary, I would argue de Botton's message is particularly valid when it comes to parenting. After all, if rituals and holidays and the veneration of certain entities have worked for thousands of years as a way to inspire hope and bring a sense of purpose to young people, why should we not use those same tactics to inspire hope and bring a sense of purpose to *our* young people? Simply because we lack religious faith doesn't mean we don't long to bring meaning to our lives, right?

If we define religion as something that helps us focus on what's important, gives our life meaning, inspires us to be better people, then it's fair to say that, in a way, we all have a religion. So what's yours?

Is it nature? Is it physics? Is it music? Art? Literature? Writing? Parenting? Yoga? Wine? (Hey, no judgment.) Sometimes identifying the things that are deeply important to your secular soul can solidify for you what you want to pass on to your children. (Okay, maybe not the wine.) Of course, your kid may not glom onto the idea of physics as easily as another kid may glom onto the idea of God. But if your kid knows, for instance, that you have existential needs and fill those needs through physics or philosophy or literature, then that can provide a reference point by which to fill their own needs.

If yours is a family that answers the Big Questions through science rather than faith, make science a central focus in your household, the way Christians make Jesus a central focus. Make a point to pick up science-centered children's books at the library. Watch nature programs on TV. Visit science museums. Listen to National Public Radio's *Radiolab* and *StarTalk* podcasts and then retell the plots and anecdotes in terms your child will understand. (My husband does this frequently with *Radiolab*. Maxine is always fascinated by the stories he tells.)

Here are some other ideas for how to reap the benefits of religious ideas in our secular families.

Holidays. Religious holidays are meant to celebrate or remember an important religious event or person. Most often they involve feasts, family, decorations, and traditions. So why not look for what's important to *you* and build a holiday celebration around *that*? Birthdays are a no-brainer, but maybe make a big deal over Martin Luther King, Jr. Day or Darwin Day, or celebrate the founding of your city or the birthday of your favorite philosopher. Or try celebrating any of these widely known holidays:

- **Inventor's Day:** February 11 (celebrates great inventors from various countries)

- **Earth Day:** April 22 (encourages environmental protection)

- **DNA Day:** April 25 (commemorates the completion of the Human Genome Project)

- **Honesty Day:** April 30 (encourages people to be honest all day long; sort of an anti-April Fool's Day)

- **Astronomy Day:** Saturday between mid-April and mid-May on or just before the first full moon (encourages interaction between astronomers and the public)

- **International Friendship Day:** July 30 (celebrates friendship)

- **Constitution Day:** The nearest weekday to September 17 (celebrates the ratification of the U.S. Constitution)

- **World Vegetarian Day:** October 1 (celebrates the ethical, environ-mental, health, and humanitarian benefits of a vegetarian lifestyle)

- **World Vegan Day:** November 1 (like Vegetarian Day, but without the cheese and butter)

- **Human Rights Day:** December 10 (commemorates the adoption of the Universal Declaration of Human Rights)

Books. We all know how important sacred texts are to the religious. There is just something about the written word that is undeniably compelling. Lots of families save the most coveted shelf space for the important sacred works in their lives—the Qur'an, for instance or the Tao de Ching or the Book of Mormon. They pick them up and refer to them often. They even set aside special days of the year to do so. So think about secular books that mean a lot to you, or that reflect values or a lifestyle that mean something to you. Create a special niche in your house for all these books, whether they be fiction, non-fiction, children's books, biographies, poetry, graphic novels, or secular parenting books(!). Remember, this is a celebration of who you are, what is important to you, and how you want to live your life. Encourage your child to read these books (when age-appropriate) and to contribute her own. And if she starts writing *her own* books to add the shelf? All the better.

Community Spirit. As de Botton humorously states in his *Religion for Atheists,* nobody ever sings with strangers anymore. And what a bummer! The community bonds created in places like churches and temples are intense. There's no reason we can't find it elsewhere. There are, of course, churches for nonbelievers; the United Universalist Church is one of them, and the up-and-coming Sunday Assembly is another. But in the absence of (or lack of interest in) literal sermons, there are plenty of other venues that offer the same type of community spirit. Seeing live performances, whether music or theater, are amazing opportunities, as are festivals, exhibits, clubs, organizations, study groups, and cultural events. My husband's preferred "church" is the Natural History Museum, which allows him to experience awe alongside his peers. He always feels as though he learns something new, gains a new appreciation for the planet, and leaves feeling wholly reinvigorated.

Charity. Muhammad Ali once told *Time* magazine: "Service to others is the rent you pay for your room here on Earth." Charity is one area that comes so naturally to so many religious believers. In Judaism, they have tzedakah. In Islam, it's zakat. So many religions make volunteerism and philanthropy an intrinsic aspect of their belief systems. For Christians, simply going to church and putting money in the collection plates can bring feelings of goodwill and selflessness. Again, though, charity is not a religious activity; all secularists can and do benefit greatly from giving their time, money, and energy to helping others. Getting kids involved in charity work as early as possible is good for everyone.

What Do You Mean Athiests Can't Pray?

The more I study world religions, the more I am struck by the threads that bind them together and how easily those threads could be rinsed of any supernatural belief and still retain meaning and purpose.

Yoga, meditation, and T'ai Chi are great examples. All are practices that were traditionally associated with religion but that have entirely secular benefits as well. Deep breathing, deep stretching, deep relaxation—all of these enhance our minds and bodies, regardless of belief.

Prayer is a religious practice that is not often secularized, but there's no reason it shouldn't be.

Not long ago, I took my daughter and a friend to a local festival where a Guatemalan family was selling its wares under a modest tent. On sale for a dollar apiece were "worry dolls," tiny, colorful dolls said to help relieve children of their worries. The kids were told to tell their worries to the dolls, tuck the dolls under their pillows, and let the dolls take away all their worries during the night. Each of the girls wanted one, and, at a buck apiece, I was happy to oblige.

Later, as Maxine and her friend excitedly palmed their new tiny friends, they began pondering the power behind them.

"I don't think it really takes your worries away," Maxine said, with a hint of disappointment in her voice. "Do you think it does, Mommy?"

I have a thing about lying when asked point-blank about something, so I told her the truth. "I don't believe in magic," I said, "so I don't think the dolls can magically take your worries away. But that doesn't mean the dolls don't work."

I explained how the very act of talking about your worries *can* actually help make them go away. Telling someone about what's bothering you—anxiety about the first day of school, the sickness of a loved one, or guilt over doing a bad thing—sometimes makes you feel better instantly. "Maybe," I told the girls, "the point of the worry doll is to give you a chance to state your worries out loud. And maybe when you do that, you really do feel better in the morning."

Maxine and her friend were more excited than ever. "I can't wait for tonight," the friend said, adding: "I have a lot of worries."

The incident got me thinking about what a service bedtime prayers—like the little worry dolls—may provide our kids. Our children have so many things on their minds that they don't necessarily want to talk about ad nauseam with their parents. But bedtime prayers, whether done privately or with mom and dad, could be opportunities for kids to verbalize their deepest thoughts, hopes, and worries; reflect quietly on their lives; and feel gratitude for all the good things in their lives.

And if, in fact, children do feel better after formally acknowledging these thoughts, it doesn't matter whether God is listening, just like it doesn't matter whether the worry doll is magic.

FROM THE BLOG
One Set of 'Footprints' is Plenty for This Kid

When I was growing up—Missouri, 1980s—half the kids I knew had a framed copy of "Footprints in the Sand" somewhere in their houses. Usually hanging in the living room.

That poem was as meaningful to these families as Rudyard Kipling's "If" was to ours. (My mom gave me a poster-sized copy of "If" sometime during my adolescent years; I must have read it 500 times.) The point is, although it wasn't in my own home, "Footprints in the Sand" was a part of my childhood. I have vivid memories of staring into pictures of sandy beaches and thinking what a comforting, beautiful sentiment that was. Or maybe it was just the thought of a beach that I found so comforting and beautiful. (This was Missouri, after all.) I assume most of you have read it, but here it is.

Footprints in the Sand

One night I dreamed I was walking along the beach with the Lord.
Many scenes from my life flashed across the sky.
In each scene I noticed footprints in the sand.
Sometimes there were two sets of footprints,
other times there was one only.
This bothered me because I noticed that during the low periods of my life,
when I was suffering from anguish,
sorrow or defeat,
I could see only one set of footprints,
so I said to the Lord,
"You promised me Lord,
that if I followed you,
you would walk with me always.
But I have noticed that during the most trying periods of my life

there has only been one set of footprints in the sand.
Why, when I needed you most, have you not been there for me?"
The Lord replied,
"The years when you have seen only one set of footprints,
my child, is when I carried you."

—author unknown

This notion of always having someone with us to keep us going is among the most common reasons people desire religious faith. It's also, I've discovered, a reason that secular parents who were raised in religious households sometimes feel guilt for not introducing their kids to this potentially friendly presence in their lives.

But telling a child that God is in the room with them may not be as compelling as it sounds. Kids' minds are far more active than ours; their imaginations are rich and vibrant. If they want or need company, they have no trouble finding it. They hug their stuffed animals. They invent imaginary friends. They cling to their blankets. They talk to themselves.

Whether or not kids think there's a God above doesn't change the fact that they must solve their own problems here on Earth. Whether we talk things through with God or with Paddington Bear has no influence on the outcome.

As of this writing, my daughter is on the fence about God—just as I was at one point, just as you may have been at one time in your own life. She is figuring things out for herself, and that makes me proud and happy.

But she said something recently that let me know, whatever she ends up believing, it will not be for lack of a second pair of footprints in the sand beside her.

"I'll never be lonely," she told me, "because I'll always have myself."

Now that, I thought, *I'd hang in my living room.*

In the absence of religion, secularists have the opportunity to rejoice in a great many things—the beauty of the world, the magic of science, the miracle of evolution, and even an appreciation for the unknowable. There is no reason we can't borrow good ideas from religion, as Alain de Botton argues, or look for ways to feed our children's innate desire for purpose and meaning and order.

Reality is a beautiful and awe-inspiring place. What we know to be true through science doesn't lessen that awe. And that we are not religious does not lesson the awe for our children. It's true that we secularists do not bestow upon our children the certainty of faith and all that goes with it. But what we can bestow may be of even greater value: a compassion for others, the ability to think for themselves, and a willingness to be wrong.

PART THREE *Dealing With Sticky Issues*

CHAPTER TEN *Grandma's Heart is Broken*

It's never easy to go against our parents' wishes. Our connection to our parents can become complicated so quickly. By the time we reach adulthood, most of us hope and expect that our parents will have made peace with our life choices and will see us as fellow adults worthy of the same respect we afford them. But that's not always the case. Some religious parents, when they become grandparents, have a tough time disengaging from their roles as teachers and influencers. Some grandparents—and aunts, uncles, and friends, for that matter—feel morally compelled to inject themselves into our children's religious educations. The result can strain relationships, even ruin them outright.

Among the non-religious parents surveyed for this book:

• **Fifty-five percent** said they had felt criticized by family and friends for raising their children in non-religious households.

• **Forty-one percent** said they felt a need to edit themselves or hide parts of their identity from people they love.

• **Thirty-four percent** feared family members would say something insensitive or harmful to their children.

• **Thirty-four percent** said they had pretended to be religious by attending church services, for example, or praying at family dinners, to avoid awkwardness, discomfort, or shame.

Most of the parents surveyed reported some degree of inter-generational tension. It can be difficult, they reported, to be sandwiched between a younger, more secular generation and an older, more rigidly religious one.

"My mother was so disappointed in me," recalled a mother from Maine. "She said she was devastated that her grandsons would grow up not knowing God. . . . It took her many months to say she loved me despite my beliefs. Even longer to say I was a good mother."

Trying to keep religion out of extended-family relationships—while keeping the love in—can be a chore, particularly when extended family members are exerting pressure to raise the children in certain ways.

Some parents surveyed said they tried to tread lightly around sensitive subjects, so their kids wouldn't inadvertently offend a grandparent or cousin. And when they felt they must contradict what children heard from relatives, they tried to phrase things in ways that would cause the least amount of friction.

"I am currently very concerned about supporting my children when they discuss these issues with my parents," one father said.

One mother said, "My children adore and look up to their grandmother who is very religious and shares her beliefs with them often. So I do worry that one day they may realize the drastic difference in our beliefs and feel they have to choose a side."

Regardless of these personal conflicts, however, most of us experience something like a gravitational pull toward our closest relatives. They are reflections of us, and we of them. They are living links to our history. No matter how much pain or frustration they cause us, the thought of pushing them out of our lives for any reason is almost always worse. We non-religious parents, like all parents, want our children to be allowed to enjoy open, meaningful relationships with extended family. We do not wish to offend or hurt anyone.

But tolerating differences of opinions can be hard in practice. On the one hand, putting our foot down on religious proselytizing may read like a cruel assault on devoutly religious relatives. On the other, if unchecked, these same relatives may pressure our kids to believe things that we don't believe are true, or may even be harmful. Some of us worry ourselves into silence.

"I don't share my own non-belief with my son," a Pennsylvania father told me, "because I am afraid that he will speak about it to my parents."

It's no wonder so many people have trouble coming out as non-religious. Being open about who we are in the face of possible adversity is a risky proposition. When the truth is out, relatives may feel disappointed, heartbroken, incredulous, guilt-ridden, fearful, or resentful. Moreover, they may feel a duty to "save" our children if we're not willing to do it ourselves. And that's a thought no one relishes.

Jennifer Newton, the secular mother we met in Chapter Two, was raised in a deeply religious household. She remembers the time she told her mother, "I just don't know what I believe anymore." Even that relatively benign statement was enough to cause her mom to break down in tears. Weeks of awkward encounters followed.

Newton remembers thinking: "This must be what coming out of the closet feels like for gay people."

Relatives Say the Darndest Things

In many families, there is no gray area. God means moral. God means good. God means heaven. Conversely, the lack of God means some truly terrible things. It's no wonder that some family members struggle with our lack of belief.

Of the parents I surveyed for this book, 49 percent said they had close family members who were religious. When asked whether they were "out" as non-religious, the highest percentage—37 percent—said they were open about their beliefs to some, but not all, thereby minimizing the tension in their lives on a case-by-case basis.

If you have close relatives who are devout believers, you may have encountered some pretty severe opposition. It's astounding the number of ignorant, condescending, manipulative, assumptive, and downright infuriating things that can come up in these conversations. Here are some of those shared with me in the survey. Feel free to highlight those you've heard yourself.

What did we do wrong?

How can you be a moral person and not believe in God?

Aren't you afraid of what will happen after you die?

Why do you hate God?

You've broken your mother's heart.

I'm sorry you've rejected God's love.

We're disappointed in you.

You don't know what you're talking about.

You're confused.

You're rebelling.

You're extreme.

You're unhappy.

You're wrong.

This is a crisis of faith.

This is a phase.

This must be part of God's plan.

You'll snap out of it.

You shouldn't tell people these things.

You're a great person . . . except for this.

I blame myself.

How can you do this to me?

It's not fair.

Even if you don't believe in God, God believes in you.

You should believe in God 'just in case.'

You've been possessed by Satan.

We'll miss you when we're in heaven and you're in hell.

We'll pray for you.

It's difficult, by the end of this list, not to notice the fever-pitch desperation at the root of so many of these remarks. As awful as some of them seem to be, most really do come from a place of love. If we can react, then, from a place of love ourselves, everyone will be better for it.

A news reporter for *Psychology Today* once asked me how I would respond to a family member who failed to grasp why I didn't believe in God. He wrote me a hypothetical letter, which said, among other things: "I like you, but I don't get you." My response to the reporter's letter could easily become my own pat response to any of the above assertions or questions, so I share it here:

> *My brain, for whatever reason, doesn't allow me to believe in God. Yours does. I can no more change the way I am than you can change the way you are. Belief is belief. If I faked it, it wouldn't be true belief. It's important that you know that I don't disbelieve as an insult to anyone. It's not a show of disrespect. I would never ask my friends or family to give up their faith. All I'm asking is the same courtesy in return. In a way, no one can truly 'get' another human being because we can't crawl inside the hearts and minds of other people. But we can promise to love each other and respect each other for all the good things we share and have in common.*

Is this the perfect comeback to any statement or question or insult thrown my way? No. But it seems to cover an awful lot of ground in a pretty darn nice way.

'My Parents are Indoctinating My Kid'

The daughter of one of my interview subjects—her name is Kelly—asked her parents for a children's Bible when she was eight. Her parents weren't religious, but saw no reason to be concerned. It seemed like natural childhood curiosity, and, frankly, her parents were happy she was showing an interest in reading. So they bought her an illustrated Bible, which Kelly proceeded to read every day for almost a year. Then one day she put the Bible on her bookshelf and never pulled it out again. That was that, or so it seemed.

Years later, when Kelly was in high school, she told her parents the reason for her brief, sudden surge in religiosity: Her mother's stepfather had told the little girl that if she didn't read the Bible every day, she'd go to hell. Her parents were dumbfounded. They couldn't believe a family member would say a thing like that—and they were horrified that they didn't know to intervene at the time.

For non-religious parents, maintaining positive, open relationships with religious relatives and in-laws can be challenging. It's one thing to maneuver around religious references at Christmas dinner or endure concerns voiced over the fate of one's soul, but it's another when relatives pressure their grown children to adopt religious customs—baptisms, communions, Bar and Bat Mitzvahs, confirmations, pilgrimages, worship rituals—so that the children, at least, can be saved from eternal damnation (or avoid reincarnation, or reach Nirvana, or any of the other alleged perks of religious belief). Even more insufferable is when a grandparent directly involves a grandchild in religious indoctrination without the parents' knowledge.

"If my mom starts dropping not-so-subtle hints about the 'Glory of God,' I can shrug it off," a California father told me. "But I'll be damned if I'll have her trying to guilt trip my son."

Another parent, a mom, told me she experienced just that.

"We've had family members try to religiously indoctrinate our child against our wishes," she said. "This has resulted in our changing guardianship in the event of our deaths."

Advice columnist Richard Wade has fielded hundreds of letters from secular people trying to manage their extended families gracefully.

"In many ways," Wade once told a reader, "dealing with religious relatives is much harder when we become parents—especially if those relatives have turned their attention to, or pinned their hopes on, our children. Sometimes grandparents may actually double down on their efforts to 'convert' our kids, having failed the first time around."

In an interview, Wade expanded on his experience.

He said it shocked him to know that the bonds of family are often overpowered by the divisive nature of religion.

"This thing," he said of religion, "is the most divisive thing ever invented by man. It divides families, neighbors, nations. It divides individuals from parts of themselves. It splits people right down the middle. It's pain on every level."

A teacher and former counselor, Wade also talked about the value of kindness when dealing with religious relatives and about how their judgment and criticisms are usually rooted in love. He talked about the uselessness of most religious debates, and the importance of treating religious relatives the way you want to be treated. In other words, if you don't want them trying to change your mind about religion, then don't try to change theirs.

That said, Wade takes a hard stand when it comes to overbearing grandparents. In another column, he addressed a single mother whose authoritarian parents were acting as her children's daycare providers while she worked. "The problem," the mother told Wade, "is that my kids are being indoctrinated with a faith that I abhor. They come home and pray at dinner, argue with me about whether Jesus really came back from the dead, and refer to my parents' church as their own. My parents are real zealots, having traveled to foreign countries to see apparitions." Wade wrote back:

> *Your parents are not villains. They think they're doing the right thing with your kids, but it is not their place to do it. They won't realize this until you explain it to them, but you're intimidated. They have developed the habit of getting their way by bullying you. Shouting, demeaning, and guilt-tripping is how they intimidate you. . . . It is time to assert your adulthood. See yourself as an adult with them, and expect respectful treatment from them. See yourself as a mother to your children, rather than a daughter to your parents.*[23]

In extreme situations, such as this, intervention is most certainly necessary. (This woman clearly needs a new babysitter!) But most situations are not extreme, and most require no more than a brief conversation with relatives about how you intend to raise your child, along with a brief conversation with your child about what their relatives believe.

So what if your in-laws send your daughter religious reading materials a couple times a year? So what if they take her to temple or read her the Qur'an or show her how to meditate in front of their Hindu shrine? As long as you've provided some scaffolding through open and honest communication with your children, none of this is likely to convince your child of anything.

And if, by chance, relatives do try to surreptitiously indoctrinate your kid, try not to panic. All other things being equal, your child is very likely to figure all this stuff out on his own anyway.

Remember Kelly, the eight-year-old who read the Bible every day for a year because her step-grandfather threatened hell if she didn't? Eventually, she closed the Bible and moved on with her life.

Why?

"She didn't see anyone in the family reading the Bible," her mother explained, "so she figured that, wherever 'hell' was, she'd be going there with the rest of her family—which didn't sound so bad."

Six Tips for Surviving Family Dinners

When raising children around devoutly religious relatives, you are almost certain to run across an awkward moment or two—or twelve. That being the case, it's important that parents who want their children to build meaningful, lasting relationships with the faith-based factions of their families be willing to make an effort. Of course, the more rigidly religious the family members are, the more effort it will take. As always, there is a balance to be struck. And, as always, love and levity can go a long way.

1. See that big chip on your shoulder? Knock it off.

Okay, so you've been disrespected, condescended to, verbally attacked, and even threatened with disownment and eternal damnation. That shit will get under anyone's skin. But if religion is ever going to become an acceptable subject among you and your relatives, you're going to have to stop taking an adversarial position. Often, we see religious exposure and treat it as religious indoctrination, or we hear words of faith and interpret them as acts of war. Shed your armor. Adopt a loving posture instead of a defensive one. Make jokes. Be self-effacing. And if all else fails, kindly change the subject to something you and your relative have in common.

2. Set your boundaries.
Know what is and what is not acceptable to you, and why. Particularly in families where grandparents are likely to proselytize to their grandchildren, boundaries need to be set. Do this in person if possible. Be nice. Make an effort to smile. Listen patiently, and try to reach an agreement with religious relatives. Let them know, gently, that you need to be able to trust that they'll abide by your decision. It's not unlike how you might already set boundaries around other issues, such as food or politics, with your extended family members. It's one thing if your mother gives your child sugar once in a while; it's another if that's all she gives her.

3. Encourage religious discussions—within reason.
People love to talk about themselves; it makes them feel good. And if your father's interests center on his religion, allowing him to talk about his beliefs is a kind and open-minded thing. Think about how touched he would be if you invited him to tell your children about his faith. He'd no longer have to sneak around you (as much), or feel (as) resentful, or worry (as intensely) that you're dragging your child to hell. When your child is old enough to separate fact from belief, let your dad know that, as long as he's not saying anything harmful, hateful, or scary, he is welcome to expose your children to his beliefs. Then give your child a context in which to hear about Grandpa's religion—or Cousin Suzie's or Neighbor Bob's. (An example: "Many people say that if you believe in Jesus, you will go to live with him in a place called heaven after you die. Grandpa believes that, which is part of the reason he wants you to believe what he does.") Just be sure to encourage your child to share what he is learning with you; that way, you can keep track of what's being said, correct misinformation, and balance things out as necessary.

4. Lower your expectations.
If you have an especially vocal family, and find yourself getting stressed out easily, you may need to lower your expectations a bit. Try promising yourself you won't get annoyed until you hear X number of religious remarks or stories. Then set the X number kind of high. I used to do this when I traveled long distances with my then-toddler. If I resolved not to get stressed until Maxine had, say, three meltdowns, then I didn't exhaust myself trying to prevent just one. My relaxed attitude made all the difference, and the trips always exceeded my expectations.

5. Avoid debate (especially when liquor is involved).
Because most of religion is faith-based, arguing about religious belief is pointless. If you find it fun to discuss or debate religious beliefs and can do so politely, then have a go at it. But if you're going to end up feeling frustrated or angry or thinking less of the person you're debating—or, worse, if you're going to hurt the other person—then leave it. Religious debate is one area where keeping your trap shut is a winning strategy.

6. If all else fails, cut ties.
Unfortunately, some relationships are just not strong enough to withstand the divide caused by religious differences. Sometimes you have family members whose rhetoric is too thick to see through or whose religious beliefs have led them to zealotry. If you no longer feel you get anything positive from a relationship, then you are within your right to limit or stop visits altogether. Just be sure you think it through first, and that you've tried your best to make the relationship work. Giving family members a chance to right their wrongs and correct their offensive behavior is a must if you are to feel good about your decision down the road.

FROM THE BLOG
When One Parent Believes, and the Other Doesn't

In America at least, mixed-religion families are becoming a norm. And that's a great thing for couples, for kids, and for society. But it comes with a fair share of complications, too. Figuring out how to talk to children about these different beliefs is one of them. It can be hard, for instance, to field questions of faith when your answers collide with those of your partner's: "Mommy's going to heaven, and Daddy is—well, he's going into the ground." But these talks (not to mention these marriages) need not end badly. The trick is to remember to love your partner the way you love your children: unconditionally. You fell in love with someone who sees the world a certain way; embrace his journey, even if you give no credence to his religious beliefs.

Here are some other things to keep in mind to make your mixed-faith marriage work to the benefit of your kids.

Speak up! Allowing one partner to take over the religious education of your child is not fair. The topic of God figures heavily into the existential questions that each and every child will explore at some point. If you can't be honest about your lack of belief, you're robbing your child of something special; you're robbing them of you.

Work out a game plan. Explain to your partner that you do not wish to denigrate their belief in any way but that you wish to share your own lack of belief with your child. Reassure your partner that you love her for being who she is, including her religious beliefs. Tell her that you want your child to be allowed to embrace her religion (as I assume, at some point, you agreed to do), but that you also want to be able to be honest about your own lack of religion. Promise each other that you won't put down the other's beliefs, but rather encourage your child to seek answers from both of you—and to be open and honest about all talks that occur when one of you is not around.

Remove "hell" from the equation. It's one thing to dangle heaven as a reward for a life well-lived; it's another to threaten hell as a punishment for non-faith. If your partner insists on telling your child that there is a fiery place where he will go if he doesn't embrace a certain set of beliefs, your partner is suffering from some major cognitive dissonance, and should be asked, as politely as possible, to back the hell off. If all else fails, remind your child that you—and billions of other people on the planet—are among those people who will supposedly be sent to hell, and that you, at least, aren't the least bit worried about it.

Encourage your child's curiosity. Your child may not know what to make of having parents with two such different attitudes toward religion at first. It might spark more questions than usual, and that's just fine. Try to answer them together as often as you can, but don't be afraid to have one-on-one talks, as well. The more your child understands that both parents will support whatever decision she makes, the less confused she will be. Also, resolve not to get upset if your child leans toward one parent's views and away from the other. (Remember, that worm turns quickly.) And, for God's sake, don't gloat!

Just the facts, ma'am. You can avoid a lot of stress with your partner (and vice versa) by just adding "I believe" in front of whatever you say. It's the concrete statements like "People who do X are disappointing God" that make non-religious parents bristle. But just adding: "It's my personal belief that . . ." or "My interpretation is . . ." to statements can go a long way toward softening them. And it's the little things that make a marriage, isn't it?

Put it on the kid. There is one refrain that works particularly well in mixed-faith marriages. One you can slide in your back pocket and pull out often. The refrain: "What makes sense to you?" Whether your child has a strong opinion on matters of faith is not important; whether his opinions are "rational" or "valid" also is not important. That your child is allowing his brain to mull over these important topics, and figure things out for himself over a period of time—that *is* important. So remember to nod and encourage and ask questions out of genuine curiosity, rather than out of a desire for a certain answer.

Acknowledge your lack of control, and embrace it. Think of your family as points on a grid, standing equidistance from one another. The goal is not to invite your child to join you on your exact point on the grid (that's never going to happen), but rather to encourage your child to be comfortable and confident on her own unique grid point. That your child is a decent person is your concern; whether she believes in the prophet Muhammad is not. If you're curious about what your kid believes, ask in the most neutral way you can: "What do you think?" And be sure she knows that however she responds is fine by you. Oftentimes, the harder you push a child to your way of thinking, the more distance the child puts between you—until, eventually, she's off your grid altogether.

It's a sad fact that religion is a divisive subject. Not only does it divide nations and neighborhoods; it divides families, too. But, when people we love and admire are sitting opposite that divide, we owe it to them, and to ourselves, to find a way over the chasm. Each family is different, of course, so the ways may vary. But, as Wade suggests, practice empathy and compassion; aim for frank, open discussions; and think long term.

CHAPTER ELEVEN *'Little Timmy's Going to Hell'*

Schoolyards are cesspools of competitive play. Kids are constantly being left out, teased, ostracized, and even bullied for traits over which they have no control. And, yes, lack of religious affiliation is one of them. Nearly 30 percent of those I surveyed said their children had suffered as a result of the family's non-belief. In many of those cases, the suffering was inflicted by peers. Some went on to explain.

> *In first grade, my daughter told her friend we didn't go to church, and the child said [my daughter] would burn in hell forever. She had nightmares for a week and was terrified to do anything.*
>
> *My son has been picked on at school by peers who come from so-called religious families for not fasting during Ramadan, for not praying regularly, etc.*
>
> *My ten-year-old has been badgered by zealous religious kids in the neighborhood who have hurt her feelings, telling her she'll go to hell because she doesn't believe. My fourteen-year-old never tells people anyone in her family might not believe in God, and implores her sister to keep quiet about it for her own 'safety.'*
>
> *Christian children have ridiculed my children at school and in the neighborhood. A ten-year-old once told my six- and eight-year-olds that 'Only kids who believe in God can play on this porch.'*
>
> *My son was picked on by classmates in kindergarten when he said that he didn't believe in God. He was told he was going to hell and was pushed by a peer on the bus.*
>
> *My girls were removed from Girl Scouts due to our pagan belief system.*
>
> *Children at school who have learned that my children do not*

believe in their god have told them that they are evil, that they are going to hell, that they are bad people. It made my children cry, and confused, because they knew that what these children said about them was not true, and they did not understand why the other children would think it at all.

My loving and kind child has had 'friends' treat him badly because he is an atheist.

That playground harassment is part of the childhood experience makes stories of religious bullying no less heartbreaking. By age six, most American children already have so much on their plates. They're juggling the pressures of school, the expectations of parents and peers, the emotional demands of growing older, and the seemingly endless list of restrictions put on their behavior. Add to that the threat of eternal damnation simply because they happened to be born into a non-religious family, and it's enough to give anyone nightmares. The good news is that these kids, like all kids who are singled out for being different, are not helpless—and neither are you.

Sticks and Stones and Threats of Damnation

It's frustrating to know that while we may do our damnedest to teach tolerance and compassion to our kids, not all parents do. In fact, many religious parents—including the parents of some of your kids' friends—lead their children to believe that it's decidedly *not okay* for people to disbelieve in Jesus or Jehovah or Allah, and that disbelievers will someday be sent to an unimaginably horrible place. It's little wonder that these stories make their way to the parks and playgrounds to be spread around.

To be fair, though, most religious parents don't teach about sin or evil or hell so that their children will go to school and taunt other kids. Far from it. Most parents are just passing on their belief systems, of which hell is a part. For very religious people, hell is an obligatory subject because hell is a *real place*—a place they don't want their children to end up, a place they don't want to end up themselves. Generally speaking, religious parents tell their kids about hell in order to encourage good behavior, moral behavior, kind behavior. That their children may use this knowledge to terrorize others is painfully ironic.

Rarely, before the age of, say, nine, do religious kids grasp the effect of their words anyway. They are just translating for their friends what they have picked up at home or in their places of worship. They may think they are imparting important information, as their religious leaders and parents did for them. Or they may be genuinely confused about why everyone is not on the same page. They also may be projecting their own fears onto your kid; they tell your kid he's going to hell for being "bad" because they're worried about going to hell for being "bad" themselves.

That's not always the case, of course. Some religious harassment happens because, well, kids are kids. Children of all ages are constantly trying to make sense of their surroundings and figure out where they fit in. They're obsessed with labels and groupings. Most, at various points in their childhood—if not throughout it!—seek to draw attention to the things that make them similar to the majority and distance themselves from the things that make them different. Often, this means pointing out things that make other people different.

Kids are singled out for being too tall or too short, for having red hair or rough hands or knobby knees or a scratchy voice or a big nose or acne. They're taunted for being too smart and for not being smart enough. They're teased for having dark skin or fair skin or talking too much or living in the wrong neighborhood or struggling with their weight or wearing hand-me-down clothes or lacking athletic abilities or having unusual interests or choosing unpopular friends.

As painful as it is, a lot of this stuff is considered developmentally appropriate. And it's not just *other kids* who do it. In all likelihood, your kid has done it, too—or will.

The Shame Game

Given the potential hurt that could be caused by religious discussions at school, the temptation may be to tell our kids not to discuss religion at all, or to keep them in the dark about our beliefs until they're old enough to exercise discretion.

I pass no judgment on those of you wanting your children to assimilate into their surroundings for their own protection. Each situation, family, and community is different. Protecting kids from harm should be a top priority. I would simply urge you to be sure you have no other alternatives. Keeping kids from your beliefs, or encouraging them to keep their beliefs from their friends, are solutions with short shelf lives.

Besides, kids *will* discuss religion with their friends; the only question is whether they'll tell you about it. If they think you'll be disappointed, worried or upset, they probably won't.

There is much to be gained from teaching kids about privacy, but be careful not to restrict children's speech by forcing privacy on them. That can send the message that you are ashamed of your views or that your kids should be ashamed of theirs.

There is absolutely no shame in being a non-religious family; letting your child think otherwise would be the real shame.

'Mommy, What's Satan?'

Of all the religious concepts we must discuss with our kids, Satan may be one of the toughest. A great way to introduce nasty but mythical ideas is by using simple, straightforward and age-appropriate language in the most matter-of-fact way that you can. So, for example, here are two ways to explain Satan to a young child.

The short answer:

"Satan is the bad guy in the Bible."

The long answer:

"In the Bible, God is the hero who wants people to be good, and Satan is the villain who tries to tempt people into being bad. (Think Batman and the Joker.) Some people—including lots of religious people—believe Satan is just a fictional character. But others believe Satan is a real being who changes forms so he can trick people into doing bad things. (Like the serpent in the Garden of Eden.) Some people think Satan is just a symbol of the bad parts of human beings—because no one is perfect, and everyone is bad sometimes. Some people believe Satan is a fallen angel who turned against God and now lives in a place called hell. You will sometimes hear people talk about 'the devil'—and that's just another word for Satan."

Dealing with Religious Harassment

You may not always be able to prevent religious harassment from happening, but you can minimize the damage, and maybe even minimize the occurrences. Here are some things you can do to help you prevent and deal with religious harassment.

Give your child a heads up. When age-appropriate to do so—around six or seven years old—let your child know that religion is a sensitive subject for a lot of people. You might say: "Religion is one of those subjects that can lead to hurt feelings. Lots of people feel very strongly about what is true and what is not true, and they get sad or even mad when people disagree with them." Then let your kids know that whether they talk about God or religion, and with whom, is entirely up to them. "But if you think you will get your feelings hurt, or someone else will, you might want to find something else to talk about."

Teach religious tolerance. If you are a non-religious person in a particularly religious community, you may not be seeing a lot of tolerance toward non-believers. But that's all the more reason to teach your own child how to treat others. Consider the following story, told by an atheist mother: "When my son was in the second grade, he made the mistake of saying something along the lines of, 'You don't really believe that baloney!' in reference to the idea that the universe was created less than 6,000 years ago. Things got ugly very quickly. By the time I got there, there were older, bigger kids pinning him in a corner and yelling at him about how he was going to be tortured in hell." There is no excuse for the actions of the bigger kids in this scenario, but the whole episode might have been prevented had the boy been informed of how important religious beliefs are to people and how showing you're nice is sometimes better than proving you're right.

Don't label your kid—or your family. You may be an atheist, agnostic, humanist, or skeptic, but your child isn't. "We do not have a 'family belief system,'" one parent told me. "We are seven individuals with individual ideas about existence." (In his book *The God Delusion*, Richard Dawkins urges against labeling children or families as "Christian" or "Muslim" before the child has a clue as to what that even means; the same holds true for non-religious labels.) When you slap a label on your child, you limit them. This is your child's exploring time. She has years and years to make up her own mind. If she wants to label herself, that's just fine, as long as she knows she can change that label any time she wants. That's the thing about being a growing kid; rapid change is inevitable. Encourage her to embrace it. That way, if she does end up discussing religion on the playground, she will be more likely to say: "I don't know what I am yet" or "I'm still exploring." And those are statements that are less likely to invite threats about hell. Again, the point is not to encourage your child to hide her true beliefs or opinions, but to make sure she knows they are hers to adopt and develop on her own.

Share religious stories and beliefs. If you live in an area where disbelief in God is treated as a bombshell, religious literacy can make a pretty effective bomb shelter. And even if it doesn't, knowing the lingo and being able to converse intelligently about different religious concepts may make your child's beliefs seem a lot less important. Shared knowledge between a religious child and a non-religious child reads a lot like shared values—at least on the surface—and that can go a long way toward cooling tension.

Don't overreact. Okay, let's say you did everything in your power to try to protect your child from the H-Bomb, but it didn't work: Someone at school has told your child he's going to hell, and your child was hurt by it—*really hurt*. First things first: Don't overreact. "Hell" is a nasty word, but it's just a word—so don't give it more weight than it's really worth. Sally is told she's "ugly" because she wears glasses or has freckles. Johnny is a "sissy" because he can't throw a ball. Mary is "retarded" because she has a stutter. Timmy is going to "hell" because he doesn't believe in God. Each insult is just as mean and hurtful as the next. Sharing stories of other children who have gone through the same thing can remind your child that she's not alone, and that there are others in the school who are probably going through the exact same thing.

Consider using it as a learning opportunity. Hell is a super-interesting field of study for kids who are old enough to handle it without nightmares. And treating it as just that—a field of study—may help remove some of its power. Google "hell." Read about how each religion imagines hell, and how they differ. You might be surprised how many religions don't envision a hell. Maybe talk to your child about how hell is depicted in songs, movies, artwork, literature, and video games. You might also explain that many people think of hell as a condition of one's own mind; when you do hurtful, amoral things, you must then suffer the guilt and remorse and regret that goes with those decisions. (For many of us, that's a fate worse than anything the devil could do!)

'Does that make sense to you?' A great centerpiece for any religiously complex conversation is this: "Does that make sense to you?" For example: "If someone is a nice person, and only does good things for other people, do you think that person will go to some horrible place after he dies? Does that make sense to you?"

Separate the hell-talkers from the religious masses. So many religious people—particularly modern, progressive types—have done away with this old-fashioned notion of hell; either they believe that only truly evil people go to hell, or they've abandoned the belief in hell altogether. And even among those who do believe in the underworld, most are not particularly worried about whether you are going to go there; they're far more worried about whether *they* are going there. The point is, not all religious people believe your kid is going to hell. Make sure your kid knows that.

Let them hurt. In this age of helicopter parenting, the idea of rescuing our children from pain is becoming all too common. But kids need to be sad sometimes, so they know that sadness passes. They need to feel disappointed, so they'll know how to deal with disappointment. They need to feel hurt so that they'll learn how to heal. Instead of trying to distract them, or talking them into feeling better, or suggesting ways to fix the situation, just be there. Sit with them in the moment. Give hugs. Let them talk if they want to. Use soothing sounds of compassion. Their hurt is real and justified, and they need to be able to deal with it in their own way and at their own pace.

If you step in, step softly. When we steer our kids too much, or expend a lot of energy trying to fix their problems, we sometimes send a message that they can't fix these problems themselves—which can kill their confidence and make them more vulnerable to playground insults. Instead, listen and encourage. If your child tells you that someone was mean to him—whether or not it was related to religion—you might say: "How did that make you feel?" or "Did you feel good about how you handled it?" (Remember, how it makes *you* feel or how *you* would have handled it is unimportant in this situation.) But, of course, sometimes kids want our help, or incidents are too serious for them to handle on their own. If a situation clearly warrants your intervention, try not to react out of anger. Treat others the way you would want to be treated if the situation were reversed. You might consider having a friendly chat with a friend's or classmate's parents, or you might send the teacher or principal of your child's school an email. In an article for the website *Parenting Beyond Belief*, blogger Steph Bazzle wrote that her eight-year-old son came home from school after a classmate told him he was headed "down there." Bazzle wrote an e-mail to the principal, teacher, and guidance counselor. Not a freak-out e-mail, she said, but a heads-up e-mail. Their response? The principal called her immediately, genuinely concerned. And the school guidance counselor scheduled a tolerance course for every grade in the school.

When the Best School is a Religious School

This is an issue that comes up *a lot* in secular families. In so many areas of our country, religious organizations have blanketed the preschool market. (I remember when I was preschool-shopping for my daughter, religious schools outnumbered Montessori-based programs five-to-one.) Sometimes, the only alternatives are religion-based.

If this is the case where you live, stay open-minded. Sending your kid to a school with religious teachings could be viewed as an opportunity for cultural education, allowing children to appreciate diversity and practice understanding. But, of course, it can be a bad thing, too—especially if parents don't do their homework beforehand or fail to closely monitor the messages their children are learning at school. And, if a kid is enrolled in any kind of a religious program, it's particularly important for parents to provide other points of view at home. If you are contemplating enrolling your child in a religious school, here are some ways to ensure it's the right decision and to minimize any surprises down the road.

Find out if you need to be religious to attend. You need not out yourself to find out the answer to this question. "Is your school open to children of different religions or of no religious affiliation?" is a question anyone could ask. Very likely, the answer is yes. And very likely, this isn't the first time they've been asked. But if the school really is "for members only," give it a pass. You don't want to put your kid in a position to have to lie—and, anyway, openly discriminatory schools don't deserve your support.

Get to know the school's curriculum. If the school is open to all children, then the next step is to find out exactly what their curriculum entails. Is it mostly secular with a few religious aspects thrown in—or is it the opposite? And what are those religious aspects? Is it simply Bible verse memorization? Or do the children pray, as well? Is hell a part of their teachings? (You want to avoid any surprises on that front). Do they teach creationism? Do they teach that you must believe in a certain way to be a good person? If you're still unsure, you might ask if you can sit in on a day or two of instruction before enrolling your child; this will give you a good sense of the place.

Find out what she's learning. If you do enroll, be sure to ask your child what she's learning in school. Ask her what stories she's hearing. Go over any religious material she brings home. And, remember, go into these conversations as a curious observer, not a private eye looking for secrets. If these conversations become too serious or stressful, your child will stop having them with you.

Double down on religious literacy. You might also say something like, "You go to a school that teaches about Jesus, but lots of other schools teach about different people," or "It's fun to learn about different religions and philosophies. Right now you are learning about the Jewish religion, but you will learn about lots of other beliefs later on." Just letting little ones know that there are other "realities" out there may be enough. For older children—those in elementary school—make religious literacy a priority. Talk about what various religions believe and why they believe those things. The more your kid knows about all religions—as well as your own beliefs—the more capable they will be to suss out the truth for themselves.

The more uncomfortable you are with the prospect of a religious school, the more thought you should give to your decision. You are the parent. You call the shots. Having someone else step in to tell your child things that you don't believe to be true *as though they are definitely true* can and probably will rub you the wrong way. So be sure the pros outweigh the cons. Yes, you may be short on other options, but maybe there's something you haven't thought of—home-schooling, for instance, or driving to a school in a nearby town, or forming a preschool co-op with other secular parents. Remember, if all secular parents put their kids in religious schools, there would never be any secular schools!

FROM THE BLOG
'Why Would God Care Whether I Believe in Him?'

Like most kids, Maxine goes through periods where she thinks quite a lot about death. She tells me from time to time that she doesn't want to lose any more of her baby teeth because that would mean she was growing up, and she doesn't want to grow up because that would mean she was getting closer to death. Pretty good logic.

Well, apparently the tooth-death thing came up at a play date because once, during a car ride when she was seven, she asked: "Is it true that people who believe in God live longer than people who don't believe in God?"

Charlie and I were a bit taken aback by the question.

"No," he answered, "that's not true."

I'm not sure if Maxine was relieved, or if the answer merely confirmed what she had suspected; but either way, she became quiet.

As I've mentioned before, Maxine is a sometimes-believer; she believes in God some days and not other days. But no matter what day it is, she speaks of God with reverence.

She would no more say something mean about God than she would kick a newborn kitten in the face. But here she was—thinking over the concept that God might take the time to punish a disbeliever by intentionally shaving years off that person's life.

Finally, she came out of her pensive state and shook her head.

"Why would God care if people believe in him?" she asked. "Why would he even care?"

And that I loved.

I remember having a similar revelation myself in my youth. God is portrayed as this big, invisible presence who never, ever shows himself to humans. How could someone like that blame a person for doubting his existence?

"If God is good," I remember telling myself, "he won't punish me for not believing."

I was eighteen years old at the time—eleven years older than Maxine was when we had this conversation. It's ironic, really, that she wants so badly to slow her growth. Because she's growing up so fast.

It can be heartbreaking to see people hurt your child's feelings, whether they mean to or not. But, if your child confronts this type of situation at some point, try to remember that religious harassment carries no more power than any other type of harassment, and focus on teaching your child to react to these situations the way you would any other type of playground bullying.

As long as your child is being true to himself, treats others the way he wants to be treated, and finds like-minded friends who can keep things in perspective, he'll come out no worse for the wear. A mother of two once told me that her children's run-ins with religious peers have actually been *good* for them.

"Sometimes pushy religious children can make school difficult," she said, "but overall our kids have developed a real backbone from this experience that is going to serve them very well in the future. Better for them to practice and build confidence at this young age and have them attract true friends who respect them and like them for who they are."

CHAPTER TWELVE *The Dog Died, Now What?*

All parents possess a fundamental instinct to protect their children from pain; that's what we do. Our arms soothe them. Our voices bring them comfort. For most of us, the very thought of being parted from our kids is anxiety-inducing in the extreme. It's often said that there is nothing worse than losing a child. And yet we all do. One way or another—through their deaths or through ours—we do.

When death comes up in conversation, it's natural to look for ways to lessen the inevitable pain of it. Most of us want so much to take the edge off, to make death less frightening. We struggle to find something—anything—to soften the harsh divide between alive and dead. As one parent put it to me: "It's the hardest subject there is." Here are some of the thoughts shared by others:

> *It is easy to tell a child that the person or pet is in heaven. It is much harder to explain how I really feel.*

> *My four-year-old asks a lot of questions about death but can't yet understand the concept of 'forever,' so it is difficult.*

> *My children have come to a belief in heaven, and during the time when they became aware of (and afraid of) death, it's comforted them to believe that I'll be waiting for them in heaven . . . and I'm not sure how to address this now in a non-crushing way.*

> *I am not sure how to discuss death without making it sound scary to such young kids. Death is scary to me as an adult, I don't want my one- and three-year-olds worrying about it, too.*

> *I'm not really sure what my own beliefs are about what happens after death. It makes it hard to answer my child's questions about it.*

> *I do believe that thinking about death is easier when you believe*

in an afterlife, but wishing doesn't make it so.

We made the mistake of calling my father 'Grandpa in Heaven.' Now we're f-ing saddled with it. It sounded better than 'Dead Grandpa' at the time.

Many parents, particularly those who grew up in religious households, find themselves turning to religious consolations: miracles, afterlife, reincarnation, and others of the sort. Describing Grandma in God's beautiful kingdom, happy and joyful and awaiting our arrival, is just so darn nice. So is picturing Fido chasing his tail up there in Doggie Heaven. Faith can feel like such an immediate salve, offering the possibility of a bright future beyond the world's greatest pain.

Faith says "yes" or "maybe" in the face of death's cold, stern "no."

But is the finality of death really a burden to our children? Is it really harder, overall, to discuss death with kids when religion is not a part of the conversation?

Heaven Doesn't Help Us

Debra Stang, a medical social worker who specializes in hospice care, has watched countless families struggle with devastating news of a loved one's imminent passing. She has hovered nearby as patients took their last breaths, and offered support as tearful goodbyes turned into unspeakable grief. Stang has seen "good deaths" and "bad deaths," and has come away with a deeper understanding of what truly comforts people in times of loss—and what doesn't.

I turned to her for advice on talking to children about death.

"It has been my experience," she told me, "that children don't respond very well to religious explanations of death, even if the family comes from a religious background. 'Grandpa's in heaven' is just too abstract for a young child, especially when he or she went to the funeral and saw Grandpa's body in a casket."

Stang's words echo those of other modern psychologists and grief experts, both religious and not.

Earl Grollman, who wrote the book *Talking about Death: A Dialogue between Parent and Child*, points out that young children are literal thinkers. Their brains haven't mastered the art of the metaphor yet, and using heaven as a "symbol" of some unspecified, abstract spiritual place may be confusing, even terrifying.[24] It's the same reason, he writes, that parents should avoid euphemisms with kids. *Passed away, taken away, resting place, went to sleep, left*—these terms are fine for adults, who know the score, but they're terrible for kids, who might be frightened to hear their loved ones have been "taken away." Instead, Grollman writes, parent would be wise to use the real words: *Die. Death. Kill. Murder. Suicide. Coffin. Cremation. Funeral.*

Miriam Jochnowitz, a parent coach and hospice volunteer, told me that religious imagery can lead to painful confusion and misunderstandings. It's not uncommon for children to hear, "Your mommy went to heaven," "God loved your baby sister so much, he took her to be with him," or "God has a plan," and take those things literally. They may wonder why Mommy would choose to go someplace without them. They may feel guilty that they didn't love their sister enough to keep her alive, or that they are being punished for not giving her enough love. They may wonder why God would make such a horrible plan, or be angry at God for breaking up their family and ignoring their most heartfelt prayers.

"One of my families," Jochnowitz said, "told a child that her deceased mother was an 'angel watching over her,' and the little girl had nightmares for months, thinking that if her mom caught her doing something wrong, she would die, too."

On top of overwhelming sadness, kids in these situations struggle with feelings of hurt, guilt, anger, fear, and confusion. Not much comfort, is it?

The idea of some type of life beyond this world is an undeniably powerful draw to human beings. Even for non-believers, that shred of hope that somewhere, somehow, the end is not really *The End* is not an easy thing to surrender. And many never do. The important thing is that, as parents, we draw a clearly delineated line between what we *believe* to be true and what we *wish* to be true.

"When it comes to death," one parent told me, "I have allowed my children to believe in a 'heaven,' for lack of a better word. I felt that allowing them to believe that 'people go on to a happy place surrounded by loved ones, waiting for other loved ones to join them someday' gives them comfort about losing people. Heck, it comforts me to make up a place like that when I am grieving also."

There's nothing wrong with wanting kids to know about all the afterlife options out there, and parents who believe in heaven should absolutely share that belief with their children. But intentionally misleading kids is not the right way out of a sensitive situation. The stakes are too high, the potential to hurt our kids too great. Take Grollman's advice: "Don't tell children what they will need to unlearn later."

The litmus test is this: Are you telling your kids something completely different than you would tell a fellow adult? If so, it's time to come clean.

Having honest, thoughtful, straight-shooting discussions about death is important. And the more we can do that while still being hopeful and positive the better. But having these clear-headed conversations becomes almost impossible in the midst of tragedy. So try to discuss death before something terrible happens. Be on the lookout for any and all excuses to have these talks. A dead bird in the yard can be a fantastic point of entry. Taking the time to explore the bird's death, what "dead" means, and why the bird died can open up those lines of communication in remarkably effective ways. Of course, many parents put off these conversations because their children are young. Each child is different, but generally kids want to hear about death much earlier than we expect. You'll know they're ready when they start asking questions: "Why is that fly not moving?" "What happened to the evil queen?" "Where did your grandma go?"

RECOMMENDED READING

Picture Books about Death

About Dying by Sara Bonnett Stein (1974). I'm crazy about this oldie, which is a book for kids and parents to read together, but also has some great information in smaller print off to the side just for the grown-ups. Best for ages five and up.

The Fall of Freddie the Leaf: A Story of Life for All Ages by Leo Buscaglia (1982). The main character in this book is a leaf who is coming to terms with the fact that he will fall (die) at some point. Good for children as young as four, this book is quite gentle and calming and would be a great introduction to death, particularly for sensitive kids who may be prone to anxiety over the subject.

The Tenth Good Thing about Barney, written by Judith Viorst and illustrated by Erik Blegvad (1987). This adorable classic is about a boy losing his cat. Such smart writing. "Barney is in the ground, and he's helping to grow flowers," the boy's father says at one point. "You know," the boys responds, "that's a pretty nice job for a cat." For ages six to nine.

When Dinosaurs Die: A Guide to Understanding Death by Laurie Krasny Brown (1998). Don't let the title turn you off. Aimed at children ages four to eight, this engaging, enlightening and forthright picture book is my daughter's favorite book about death—and mine.

When a Pet Dies by Fred Rogers (1998). Did Mr. Rogers ever do anything that wasn't awesome? No. No, he didn't. For ages five to eight.

Comforting Kids Without Religion

It's been my experience that the reason so many parents falter when it comes to these talks about death is because, without religion, they are left with a void to fill. They want to help reduce their children's anxiety about death (and their own!), but don't know where to turn. ("If I can't talk about heaven, then there's nothing left to say.") But that's not true. Heaven isn't the only tool in the toolbox. There are other things we can give them.

1. Give them science.

Adults tend to focus their worry on the emotional aspects of death—how it feels to lose someone we love, how we would cope without them. But children of a certain age—particularly preschoolers—aren't as consumed by the grief aspect of death. Focusing on the science of death is a great way to normalize death discussions for you both, and give you a solid foundation for speaking about death as a natural phenomenon, rather than a terrifying inevitability.

Talking about decomposing bodies may, at first, seem ghoulish, but the actual science of death is not only fascinating to children, but can be comforting, too. Kids are still figuring out how things die ("Could I have caused it?") and how it feels to be dead ("Will I be lonely?"). This is precisely why it's so important to explain to kids how we humans work—how our beating hearts are what keep us alive, and that there is a difference between bodies and consciousness.

"Most children understand the concept of something that has 'stopped working completely and can't be fixed,'" Stang says. "It's also important to reassure children that a dead person doesn't breathe, wake up, go to sleep, or need to go to the bathroom, doesn't hear or see anything, doesn't get hungry or cold or scared, and doesn't feel any pain."

Reminding a child that everything ends and dies, and that this is the nature of the universe, can and does help, adds Eve Eliot, a psychotherapist and yoga teacher living in New York. For example, she often cites "the end of the day when the sun goes down, the disappearance of the dinosaurs, the time in (kids') lives when they have to leave the comfort of being home with their moms and enter school for the very first time. The very next inhale will be 'lost on the very next exhale.'"

Many parents I surveyed had embraced this way of thinking about death—with great success.

One Washington mother had this to say:

> *We're just very matter-of-fact about how the body works, how it sometimes stops working and causes death, especially once we get old, and what we do with the body once it is non-functional—how it degrades and becomes part of the earth again. My son has a pretty firm grasp on death, to the best of his five-year-old ability. Recently a religious aunt said about a recently passed relative: 'Great uncle Johnny went on to the next life,' and my son said sympathetically, 'Yeah, his next life underground.'*

Do remember, of course, that there is a limit to how much science to impose on a young child. "It can be helpful just to understand more about what happened," Jochnowitz advised. "But follow the child's lead. Do not expound if they are not interested."

2. Give them attention.

Many children, for whatever reason, go through a death-obsession stage. They worry about their parents' dying, or themselves. For these kids especially, parents would be wise to ask open-ended questions, encourage children to talk about their fears, and to assure these kids that, just as death is natural, so too is the *fear* of death.

"It's okay to think about death and to be scared of it," you might say. "That's what helps keep us from doing things that threaten our health and safety. What things can you think of that will help you to live a long, long life?"

Understanding the finality of death is a sign of growing up, and talking about all the things that help keep people alive—eating right, exercising, getting medical checkups, looking both ways when you cross the street—can be a great way to redirect a child's anxiety into something positive.

Engaging with children about these fears, as opposed to trying to keep the fears at bay, will help them follow these thoughts to their logical conclusions.

"What if you die?" your child might ask.

"Yes, what if I die?" you could say. "What would that be like?"

Such prompts might lead to thoughts that surprise you. "Will I have to live in an orphanage?" your child might ask. Or "Who will kiss me goodnight?"

But as great as talking prompts can be, one of the best things you can do is listen. Instead of trying to identify a way to make the pain stop, just be present. Nods and hugs are fine, but parents who try too hard to comfort with words can end up explaining more than a child wants or is ready to hear. When in doubt, try turning the questions back on the child. Grollman offers this example: When a child asks, "What did Grandma look like after she died?" a parent might answer: "What do you think she looked like?" This may offer some insight into the child's imagination and help guide the conversation where it needs to go.

3. Give them confidence.

One thing that surprised me, as I researched this book, was that psychological research has all but debunked Elisabeth Kubler-Ross' "Five Stages of Grief," which was made famous in her 1969 bestselling book, *On Death and Dying*. In fact, when it comes to losing a loved one, grief doesn't work in "stages" at all. In his enlightening book, *The Other Side of Sadness: What the New Science of Bereavement Tells Us About Life After Loss*, author George Bonanno writes that resilience—not denial, anger, bargaining, depression and acceptance—is what truly defines loss and grief.[25] His scientific studies, conducted over 20 years, show that most people weather the deaths of loved ones relatively quickly and thoroughly. Mere weeks after devastating losses, many people are able to experience genuinely positive emotions, even laughter. And this is not denial or drugs doing the work—but rather our own natural resiliency, Bonanno writes.

Personality has a lot to do with grief reactions, of course, and some do experience grief in the Kubler-Ross-created image. But, in general, studies show, grief has an oscillating pattern. It comes and goes in "waves," which is what, mercifully, allows us to take care of ourselves and those around us.

I tell you this because, sometimes, our fear of death comes down to the fear of grief. We fear that losing our loved ones will leave us sad forever. That we'll never laugh as loud or as long, that we'll forever be damaged by our loss. But Bonanno's message is one many children could benefit from hearing: Our bodies are hardwired to adapt, we are stronger than we think we are, and the world is an endless source of love and joy. This is an assurance worth having—and worth giving.

4. Give them practice (and an outlet).

A side benefit to keeping pets is to familiarize kids with the idea of death, to let them practice mourning, and to remind them that life goes on after loved ones die. But, so often, we shield our children from the death of pets and, therefore, miss opportunities to let our kids build up their own coping mechanisms.

By encouraging your children to be present when your pets are euthanized and/or allowing your children to be involved in the mourning process with you (rather than, say, leaving the room to cry), you are teaching your kids how to mourn and move on. You are teaching them it's okay to cry, and that grief—no matter how painful—is not life-threatening.

Likewise, invite your children to participate in mourning rituals when family members die. Modern therapists not only condone taking young children to funerals; they encourage it. Unless the child refuses to go (which rarely happens, I'm told), young kids should be able to witness and partici- pate in the catharsis that funerals bring. Also, children need confirmation of death much more so than adults do. Without it, they may view death as something mysterious and temporary, rather than a real, permanent state. They may even await a loved one's return.

"Participation helps soften the pain, enhance the healing process, and provide an opportunity for acceptance and transformation," said Lynn Isenberg, co-author of the book *Grief Wellness: The Definitive Guide to Dealing with Loss.*

"When a child can participate in a loved one's passing," Isenberg said in an interview, "it creates an action, a sense of doing, a sense of purpose, around the loss. A child can plan a ceremony, create a ritual, write words to share with family and/or friends, design an activity around healing—especially if the activity was directly related to the person who has died."

Also, be sure to give children outlets for their mourning. Poetry and song-writing are outlets. Exercise is an outlet. Therapy is *definitely* an outlet. Outlets are not distractions—that is, activities aimed to keep our minds off the pain. Outlets are things we can do while working through our emotions. Encouraging kids to "feel their feelings" is important—even when those feelings are very bad or sad.

5. Give them permission to be sad.

Russell Friedman, co-founder of the Grief Recovery Institute in Sherman Oaks, California, has spent nearly three decades counseling people in the midst of grief. Friedman talks a lot about the myth that it is both good and helpful to comfort grieving people.

Sadness, Friedman told me, is such a healthy emotion at times of devastating loss. It's appropriate. And trying to remove the sadness when someone is grieving is both inappropriate and unhealthy.

To make his point, Friedman pointed to the emotion of happiness. Would we ever tell a loved one that they ought to feel less happy about a job offer because they might lose that job some day? Would we tell someone to not feel so good about their engagement because 50 percent of marriages end in divorce?

Of course not. So why do we rush to relieve people of their sadness or discomfort when those feelings are totally suitable for the occasion?

"Parents," Friedman said, "tend to use heaven to get children not to feel bad at a time when it's natural and healthy to feel bad. . . . Why aren't we allowed to be sad when sad is the emotion of the day? Why is comfort the goal?"

I must admit, this small piece of insight was kind of a game-changer for me personally. Before that, I always had a natural inclination to want to make people feel better. And I always felt proud when I was able to do that. It had never occurred to me, until I talked to Friedman, that in my quest to keep sadness at bay at times of loss, I might have been cutting off someone else's rightful, natural grief. Or my own.

6. Give them permission to be happy.

After a person dies, the only thing we have left of them is our memories. Yet so many of us don't talk about dead people because we feel even our happiest memories lead us to melancholy. We assume the only way to avoid the painful end is to not begin at all. But honoring our dead and keeping them with us is part of how we cope with our losses. Suppressing those memories can deprive us of both joy and comfort. As I said above, working Grandma's favorite recipe into a mealtime, telling Grandpa's favorite joke, or recounting the copious amounts of liquor Great Aunt Tilly used to consume at Passover every year are all healthy ways of coping—not just with *their* deaths, but with death in general. Giving memories of our dead a happy place among the living benefits us all. Especially our kids.

Yes, there is something undeniably poetic about the idea of heaven. But non-belief can be poetic, too. Maybe you believe, as I do, that, after we die, people simply go back to the same non-existence they experienced (or didn't experience) before they were born. Maybe you believe that we become memories—not souls—and that the point of living isn't to get somewhere else but to collect memories that make us happy and give memories that make other people happy. Being a good person, the central focus of most major religions, is vital in this scenario because other peoples' memories are the last vestiges of ourselves. And if their memories of us will be the only part of us left after we die, then our purpose is to make those memories as good as we possibly can.

FROM THE BLOG

Matt Logelin—Widower, Dad, Non-Believer

You may have heard of Matt Logelin. He's a blogger and author whose wife, Liz, died the day after delivering the couple's first child in March 2008.

The child, a baby girl named Madeline, had been born seven weeks premature and was being cared for in the ICU while Liz remained on bed rest for 24 hours. Given the go-ahead to finally hold Madeline, Liz excitedly rose from her hospital bed, sat down in a wheelchair, complained of being light-headed, and died of a pulmonary embolism.

The story is tragic, but Matt's blog—which he began before his wife's death—is fascinating and somehow manages to be surprisingly uplifting. Matt wrote a book called *Two Kisses for Maddy: A Memoir of Loss & Love* in which he recounts the strange and surreal collision of birth and death in a 27-hour period.

I interviewed Matt after I learned he, too, was a non-religious parent. Matt described himself to me as a lapsed Catholic, explaining that he lost his faith in God somewhere around age seven, after hearing that a friend of his—a Hindu boy—was going to go to hell because he didn't believe in Jesus.

The boy's family was really nice, Matt said, and he remembers thinking: "That's not okay. That's really awful."

It's hard to imagine anything tougher than caring for a newborn while mourning the loss of your wife. It's hard to imagine how painful it must have been to look at his daughter in the eyes and tell her that she was never, ever going to meet her mother. Not ever.

But that's exactly what Matt did.

From the time Madeline was days old, in fact, Matt began talking to her about Liz's death—using the same words he would use with an adult. He steered clear of euphemisms. He didn't try to offer explanations where none existed. He talked about Liz in the past tense.

"Your mom died," he told her during those first weeks, and again dozens of times after that. "That means she's not here. She gave birth to you. She loved you, and she was really excited to hold you."

He said it felt good to know that this narrative, this message, would be consistent as she got older. There would be no confusion, no surprises.

Today, Maddie is doing great. A little, towheaded beauty, she's healthy, well-adjusted, spirited, and funny. And Matt, too, has managed to move forward. He is a happy, devoted father.

But, of course, it's clear from his blog posts that he'll never break completely free of the sadness of his loss. Hell, even if he *were* inclined to forget Liz, it would never happen. One need only to look at his daughter to understand why.

Maddie, as fate would have it, is a spitting image of her mother.

Heaven is a belief. And just like all beliefs, your child will decide for herself whether that concept fits into her worldview; there is no need to push in either direction. But it's important that she understands—as you presumably do—that dying is as natural as living; that death is as painless as sleep; and that a rich, rewarding life full of meaning, hope and joy is contingent on your attitude in life, not your ability to acquire immortality after death.

This life is wondrous enough—if only we let it be.

CONCLUSION

We live in an unusual time in our history. We see secularism clearly on the rise, and yet religious beliefs influence society as much as ever. Some authorities tell us that God is on the way out; others tell us that God is on the way up. It's hard to know where we stand, where the country stands, and what the future holds.

For those who have turned away from faith or become accustomed to ignoring religion, the thought of discussing these sensitive matters with children can weigh heavily. Being objective about things we think are flat-out untrue may seem impossible—even unnecessary.

Shortly after I decided to write this book, I reached out to the communications director of an atheist group in New York. I told her about my project and asked her if I could interview some parents in her group about how they had gone about introducing their children to religion.

Her response was short and curt.

"As an atheist," she wrote, "I did not introduce my children to religion. And nobody I know [in this group] would introduce their kids to religion."

That e-mail has become a touchstone for me—a reminder of what is missing from secular parenting in this country today. This idea that we, as parents, bear no responsibility for introducing our kids to the beliefs we don't personally value is all too common. But as we've seen, it's unrealistic to think that we can keep our children out of religion simply by not mentioning it. Disparaging or ignoring faith, or treating faith as though it doesn't matter, is so very shortsighted. We let our fears and apathy guide us, rather than our common sense, and we let our own opinions blind us to what really matters—raising our kids to be kind to one another.

Secularism has a foothold in our society and is sure to grow in the decades ahead. Science isn't going away, and neither is the Internet. As long as we continue to discover more about the world, and about each other, religious affiliations will loosen. At least that's my prediction—my *belief*, if you will—based on nothing more than my own meager research and a strong gut instinct. (Hey, we all have a right to our beliefs!)

I know that some people see religion as a threat, and some religious people *can* pose threats. But, in our role as parents, and in light of America's secular boom, perhaps religion is not the threat we should be worried about; perhaps *bigotry* is.

As parents on the front lines of this great shift, we have an opportunity to make sure that disbelief doesn't translate into unkind, disdainful, or condescending comments about people who mean us no harm. Knowing ourselves and our biases, tamping down our inner vitriol, and maintaining some humility are crucial first steps.

Instead of being concerned with whether our kids believe in the existence of God or Krishna or Santa Claus or Batman, let's focus on whether we are raising our kids to see people as individuals with a range of experiences, emotions, and reasons for believing what they believe. Let's teach our kids to search for and find what they have in common with people, not to ridicule anyone's personal truths as "stupid" or "silly," or to make broad (and nasty) generalizations about decent people. Yes, religious people may be annoyingly opinionated at times; I can be, too. And so can you, I bet. Yes, religious people may really, really want you to agree with them. (Just like I really, really want you to agree with me right now!)

But none of that should make or break a relationship. If—outside the subject of religion—two people like, respect, and trust each other—that's what's important.

When we let our kids believe whatever they want, we allow them to be in the drivers' seats of their own destinies—which is, of course, precisely the way it should be.

Prayer, like sex, is something people do. Someday your child might do it, too. She might even enjoy it. So take a deep breath and practice talking about religion without judgment. Talk about it the way you might talk about, say, the Notre Dame Cathedral in Paris. Notre Dame is a church, yes. But it's also a beautiful building to be explored and appreciated on numerous levels. Don't make your child go inside it alone. Hold her hand. Explain what you can. Enjoy the view. If she chooses to bow her head and pray, sit lovingly with her while she does. In all likelihood, she'll eventually rise from the pew, clasp your hand once again, and return with you into the sunlight.

It has been four years since that conversation with my daughter in the car—the one where she told me that God made her and my brain flatlined. I've learned a lot since then. Without the self-imposed pressure to keep Maxine "within the yellow lines" of my own belief system, I am now free to make the business of religious literacy a laid-back, leisurely affair, rather than an anxiety-inducing one. It has opened the door for us to celebrate all sorts of religious holidays, and to speak openly and candidly with our loved ones about a wide range of customs, stories, events, and beliefs.

I have been most touched, in fact, by the response I've received to this book by my own religious friends and family members. Almost without exception, they have reacted to my work with genuine curiosity, if not wholehearted support. And some of them have even encouraged their own children to ask me about my atheism and find out why I lack religious belief. This, to me, is tolerance in the best sense, and it never fails to bring tears to my eyes—because it means these friends are affording me and my worldview the same respect I am affording them and theirs.

In this way, and many others, talking about religion has turned into one of the most rewarding experiences of my life.

As non-religious parents, you are guaranteed to field a lot of tough questions. The answers may not come naturally to you at first, and the discussions that follow may not always be easy or pleasant. But relax . . . it's just God. With a bit of forethought, you, too, can offer your child honest answers to his questions while also guiding him to think critically, reach his own conclusions, and develop compassion and understanding for those who believe differently than he does. And, in doing so, you can help leave the world just a little bit better than you found it.

When my daughter informed me, at the age of five, that God made her, I didn't know what to say. But I do now.

I hope you do, too.

APPENDIX

Cheat Sheet to World Religions (and Holiday Guide)

This cheat sheet represents five of the world's most popular religions, along with some associated holidays. I have tried to summarize and simplify these religions without sacrificing accuracy, but if you see any mistakes, I encourage you to report them to:
relaxitsjustgod@gmail.com.

HINDUISM

Founded: In the vicinity of 2500-1500 BCE
Deities: Brahman is considered to be the supreme spirit that created the world, but he is said to inhabit a trinity of gods: Brahma (the creator), Vishnu (the preserver), and Shiva (the destroyer). Each of these gods, in turn, inhabit many other lords and avatars—including Krishna, Goddess Lakshmi, and Buddha (yes, *that* Buddha.)
Famous Dogma: Karma will catch up with all people—in this life or the next.
Methods of Worship: Mantras, music, meditation, prayer, yoga, and offerings of food and firewood. Temple visits may occur anytime. Worship (puja) also occurs regularly at household shrines.
Symbol: Om (a sacred incantation intoned before or after sacred readings, prayers, or mantras)
Major Sects: Vaishnavism, Shaivism, Shaktism, Smartism, and the Hare Krishna movement
Number of Followers: One billion
Sacred Texts: The Four Vedas, the Mahabharata (of which the Bhagavad Gita is a part), and Ramayana
Life-Cycle Celebrations: Thread ceremonies, marriages, pilgrimages to the Himalayas, funeral rites, and last sacraments
Traditional Views of Afterlife: Early Vedic tradition spoke of a heavenly world of the ancestors, but Hindus seek Moksha—which is

when Hindus break free of the endless cycle of reincarnation and unite with Brahman.
Clothing: For women, simple but elegant draped (and midriff-baring) garments called saris, head scarves, and bindis (forehead dots); for men, kurta pajamas and possibly shawls that can be wrapped around their shoulders
Major Narrative: For hundreds of centuries, the people of India practiced ancient Vedic religions, which centered on worshiping natural elements (like fire and rivers) in addition to a pantheon of gods. Out of this evolved Hinduism, which offered a new possibility—that people were reincarnated into other bodies after they died. It was said that people were reborn into higher or lower social castes depending on how good they had been during their lives, but that the ultimate goal was Moksha—to escape the endless cycle of death and rebirth through at least one of four avenues: knowledge/wisdom, right action/good deeds, meditation/yoga, or total devotion to one of many Hindu gods or goddesses. Although there is no overarching narrative—Hinduism is too old for that—we do know that the story of Lord Rama is all-important in Hinduism. As evidenced in its holiday traditions, Hinduism is a relatively playful religion—lively, happy and colorful—especially in contrast to the serious, solemn and sometimes sad aspects of monotheistic religions.
Important Holidays: Holi, Diwali (detailed below), Hivaratri

Diwali
Pronounced: Di-VAH-li
AKA: Festival of Lights
Religion Represented: Hinduism
Date: Corresponds with the new moon that falls between the 7th and 8th months of the Hindu lunisolar calendar
Celebrates: The Hindu New Year
Star of the Show: Lord Rama
Back Story: Diwali celebrates the conquest of good over evil. There are lots of legends of how it began, but one of the most common is that Lord Rama—said to be an incarnation of the supreme god Vishnu—was exiled from his father's kingdom for fourteen years. While in exile, Rama's wife was kidnapped, precipitating an epic journey to rescue her and defeat her demon captors. Following Rama's victory, he returned to the kingdom to be crowned king and, eventually, emperor. His

rule was a time of joy, peace, and prosperity, and his people marked the happy homecoming by lighting rows of clay lamps, setting off fireworks, and celebrating with family.
Associated Literary Passages: This story of Lord Rama is part of the Ramayana, one of the longest poems ever written and a "national epic of India."
The Food and Fun: There is not a set menu for Diwali, but dinner tends to be elaborate and vegetarian: curry, samosas, paneer, sabzi, rice, and naan. And sweets are a necessity, so there are plenty of desserts. Diwali celebrants often give their houses a deep cleaning, decorate their front doors, and leave their wallets out during parties to encourage Lakshmi, the goddess of wealth, to enter the home and bring them—what else?—wealth. They also light firecrackers, dance to Bollywood music, and play poker late into the night. Oh, and you are required—REQUIRED—to wear new clothes. (Where do I sign up?)
Conveying Meaning to Kids: Consider throwing a Diwali party. Tell the Wikipedia-version of the Rama story, program your Pandora to Classic Bollywood, and let your child decorate the front door. Light as many candles as you can find (remember it's a festival of lights!), serve Indian food and sweets, and break out the playing cards for a few games of Go-Fish or, depending on the age/gambling penchant of the child, a little Five-Card Stud. And don't forget *Amma, Tell me About Diwali!* by Bhakti Mathur.

JUDAISM

Founded: In the neighborhood of 1300 BCE
Deity: God
Famous Dogma: God established a covenant with the Jewish people that made them God's sacred, or chosen, children.
Methods of Worship: Prayer, singing, reciting the Torah, and attending synagogue. The Jewish Sabbath (day of rest) lasts from Friday evening to Saturday evening and is often referred to as Shabbat.
Symbol: Star of David
Major Sects: Orthodox, Conservative, Reform, Reconstructionist

Number of Followers: Fourteen million
Sacred Texts: The Torah (Genesis, Exodus, Leviticus, Deuteronomy, and Numbers), as well as the Talmud and Mishnah (both of which offer rabbinical, legal, and narrative interpretations of the Torah). The Nevi'im and Ketuvim are the books of history, prophecy, poetry, and other sacred writings that combine with the Torah to form the Hebrew Bible (Tanakh).
Life-Cycle Celebrations: Bris (circumcision) and Bar Mitzvahs for boys, baby namings and Bat Mitzvahs for girls, weddings, pilgrimages to Israel, and funerals
Traditional Views of Afterlife: The place of spiritual reward for the righteous dead in Judaism is referred to as the World to Come or the Garden of Eden, but there is no vivid description of these places. The Hebrew Bible refers to the coming of the Mashiach (Messiah), a man who will be chosen by God to put an end to all evil in the world, rebuild the temple, bring the exiles back to Israel, and usher in a time of global peace. Whether this should be interpreted as an afterlife is open to debate.
Clothing: Men wear skullcaps called kippahs, also called yarmulkes. (Orthodox men wear them all the time; other sects wear them only for prayer.) Strictly observant Jewish men commonly wear "little tallits"—which are four-cornered garments, similar to ponchos—under their shirts. Orthodox Jewish men are known to wear side curls and untrimmed beards—both a result of literal interpretations of the Torah. Married women may cover their hair.
Major Narrative: Judaism is one of the oldest monotheistic religions practiced today. Prior to Judaism, ancient Israel was inhabited by people who worshipped many gods. The idea that there was only one God was relatively new at the time. The single most important narrative in Jewish tradition is told in the Torah's Book of Exodus. As the story goes, thousands of ancient Jews (Israelites) were living as slaves in Egypt. A cruel Egyptian pharaoh ordered all the Israelite's eldest sons to be murdered, which infuriated God—who proclaimed that Israel was God's firstborn son (making the Israelites his chosen children). God approached Moses at the legendary burning bush to lead the Israelites out of Egypt, and Moses accepted. "Let my people go," Moses told the pharaoh, over and over again. But the pharaoh refused, even after God infected all of Egypt with nine of ten horrific plagues. The last and worst plague was that God would kill the firstborn sons of all Egyptians. He warned the Israelites ahead of time to put lamb's blood in

front of their doors, so the angel of death would know to "pass over" those houses and thus spare their sons. It was then that the pharaoh consented to let the Jews leave, and leave they did—so fast, Exodus tells us, that their bread didn't even have time to rise. (Fortuitous, really, since crackers make much better travelers than bread anyway.) When the pharaoh changed his mind and ordered his army to recapture the Israelites, Moses (again, legendarily) parted the Red Sea with his magical staff, which led his people to freedom and drowned all pursuers in their wake. They wandered the desert for forty years before finally returning to their homeland.

Important Holidays: Rosh Hashanah and Yom Kippur (detailed below) signal the beginning and end of Judaism's ten "High Holy Days," but there are twelve major holidays—including Passover (also detailed below), Purim, and Hanukkah.

Rosh Hashanah and Yom Kippur

Pronounced: ROE-sha-SHA-na and Yom Ki-POOR

AKA: The Jewish New Year and The Day of Atonement

Religion Represented: Judaism

Date: The ten High Holy Days—book-ended by Rosh Hashanah and Yom Kippur—are the first ten days of the Hebrew month of Tishrei.

Star of the Show: God

Back Story: Yom Kippur is slightly more important than Rosh Hashanah, but the two are intricately tied together. The period in between is a time of mending fences and reflecting on things that one can do to improve himself or herself from the previous year. It's said that on Rosh Hashanah you'll either be written in or out of the "Book of Life" for the coming year, but that on Yom Kippur, the book is sealed—meaning you've got that time in between to screw up or make your righteousness known. More than anything, Yom Kippur is a day of seeking forgiveness and giving to charity.

Associated Literary Passages: Leviticus 16:29 and 23:27, Numbers 29:7-11, and Mishnah Tract Yomah 8:1

The Food and Fun: Foodwise, Rosh Hashana is associated with apples and honey (symbolizing a sweet new year), as well as pomegranates and challah (braided bread). In lieu of silly hats and tasseled squawkers, celebrants sport the traditional yarmulke and blow a cool-looking horn called a shofar.

Yom Kippur, on the other hand, is a time of fasting—no food or fun!—and is considered a solemn occasion. (It's not appropriate, for instance, to wish people a "Happy Yom Kippur.") Often called the "Sabbath of all Sabbaths," Yom Kippur is not only a day of fasting and complete rest (no working) but also of other restrictions—no washing or bathing, no perfumes or deodorants, no wearing leather shoes, and no sex. Services run all day on Yom Kippur—from 8 a.m. to 6 p.m.—with a break around 3 p.m. People wear white, and services generally end with a long blow from the shofar.

Conveying Meaning to Kids: Explain to kids that Rosh Hashanah is a time for reflecting on your life and challenging yourself to become a better human being. Serve apples and pomegranates with dinner and ask your familly members to come up with ways in which they might improve themselves; then have everyone commit to doing it. Then, on Yom Kippur, check in with everyone about how well they did. Also, Yom Kippur is a great opportunity to explain to kids the meaning of a "Sabbath"—or day of rest. You might share the Biblical creation story about how God made the world in six days and then rested on the seventh, and how many religious people believe that one day out of each week should be set aside to rest and think about God. Some religious people have their Sabbaths on Saturday, some on Sunday. Friday is the traditional day of prayer for Muslims, and Buddhists have a day of rest every seventh or eighth day. If you live in the United States, you might share with your children that the Sabbath is the reason people generally get weekends off of school, and then chat about how important rest and relaxation is to all human beings, religious or not.

Passover

AKA: "Feast of the Unleavened Bread"

Religion Represented: Judaism

Celebrates: The exodus of the ancient Jewish people from Egyptian slavery

Date: The 15th to 21st day in the Hebrew month of Nisan

Star of the Show: Moses

Back Story: The Torah's Book of Exodus recounts the story of the ancient Jews (Israelites) who were living as slaves in

Egypt. [See major narrative of Judaism above.]
Associated Literary Passages: Exodus 3:1-15:26, Leviticus 23:1-15, Numbers 9:1-15, The Babylonian Talmud: Tract Pesachim, and the Union Haggadah
The Food and Fun: It wouldn't be Passover without unleavened bread, called matzah. But there are other symbolic foods, too: bitter herbs (to symbolize the bitterness of slavery); a mixture of apples, nuts, wine, and cinnamon (to symbolize the mortar Jewish slaves used to build Egyptian cities); a roasted egg (perpetual existence); vegetables (new life and hope); salt water (tears shed during slavery); and roasted lamb (the blood over the doorways). Oh, and observers must—must!—consume four glasses of wine over the course of the dinner, which represent the four-fold promise of redemption. Specific Seder rituals are all laid out in the Haggadah. (And, yes, in case you were wondering, there *is* an app for that.) Observers eat and drink in a certain order; recite the Passover story; invite children to ask "four questions" about Passover; sing songs; and hide the afikoman, which is a piece of matzah in a napkin that the kids must find and then share with everyone. Observers also pour an extra glass of wine and leave the door open in case Elijah the prophet arrives. (Spoiler alert: He never does.)
Conveying Meaning to Kids: Because Passover was, in a sense, created to introduce Judaism to children, there are tons of cute Passover children's books, some that focus on the backstory, others that focus on the traditions of the Seder. Both kinds are absolutely worth checking out, although some are more neutral than others. You can always hold a quasi-Seder, of course, telling your child the Exodus story and then serving the symbolic food and talking about what each means. In addition to *Passover* by Miriam Nerlove, also check out *Let My People Go* by Tilda Balsley and *Passover: Celebrating Now, Remembering Then* by Harriet Ziefert.

BUDDHISM

Founded: In the vicinity of 500 BCE
Deity: None
Famous Dogma: Siddhartha Guatama, also known as the Buddha, discovered a way to end suffering through the cessation of all desire.
Methods of Worship: Chants, music, meditation, yoga, salutations, incense, and offerings of food. "Worship" is a bit of a misnomer here—as the Buddha is said to be honored, not worshipped. Temple and monastery visits may occur anytime. Buddhists have household shrines, as well.
Symbol: Wheel of Life
Major Sects: Theravada, Mahayana, Zen, and Tibetan
Number of Followers: 500 million
Sacred Texts: Jataka (a collection of fables framed as previous incarnations of the Buddha) and the Tripitaka (Buddhist cannon that contains teachings of the Buddha, interpretations of Buddhist doctrine, and written rules for monastic life)
Most Important Rules: The Five Precepts, Four Noble Truths, and the Eightfold Path
Life-Cycle Celebrations: Confirmation rites (receiving a Buddhist name), becoming a monk or nun for a period of time, and funeral services
Traditional Views of Afterlife: In Buddhism, there are many realms of heaven, each based on karma and none of them permanent. Because Buddhism grew out of Hinduism, there remains a belief in reincarnation, but Buddhists focus much more on attaining Enlightenment (Nirvana) as a way to end the death-rebirth cycle.
Clothing: Buddhist monks and nuns wear toga-like robes in a variety of colors and shave their heads. (All Buddhist men are expected to become a monk at some point in their lives.)
Major Narrative: Siddhartha Guatama was the Hindu-born son of an Indian king born somewhere between 400 and 560 BCE. Although stories of his birth vary, most sacred texts hold that Siddhartha was born in a field in the foothills of the Himalayas. He was said to have magically sprung from his mother's side, bathed in golden light. Siddhartha's mother died only days later, and Siddhartha was raised by his father and his aunt inside the sprawling walls of the king's palace. As the story goes, he did not see pain or suffering—illness, old age, death—until he was well into adulthood. Troubled by the truth of

it all, he left his home, wife, and baby in search of an end to earthly suffering. For years, he wandered his country, meditating and fasting and living the traditional, poverty-stricken life of an ascetic. Finally, very near death and sitting beneath a Bodhi tree, Siddhartha became the Buddha (the "Enlightened One"). How? Well, in a nutshell, he realized that the cause of all suffering was desire, cravings, and our attachment to people, places, and things. He said the cessation of suffering was attainable through the release of all desire or cravings, and then he devised of a way to do that. This he called the Noble Eightfold Path, which amounts to pieces of wisdom that, if put into practice, is sure to generate happiness, if not Nirvana. The Buddha spent the next forty to fifty years teaching about the Eightfold Path, so that others could practice it for themselves. Much revered, Buddha died at the ripe old age of eighty(ish.)

Important Holidays: Vesak (detailed below), Bodhi Day, Observance Day, and Sangha Day

Vesak

Pronounced: VEE-sak

AKA: Wesak or Veskha

Religion Represented: Buddhism

Date: Most countries celebrate Vesak on the 15th day of the fourth month in the Chinese lunar calendar.

Celebrates: The life, enlightenment, and death of the Buddha

Star of the Show: Buddha

Back Story: According to scripture, the Buddha was sitting beneath a Bodhi tree, meditating, when he devised the Four Noble Truths (the cause of all human suffering) and the Noble Eightfold Path (the solution). This is what is referred to as his Enlightenment. His realization was rather simple: If people followed the Eightfold Path, they could eliminate their suffering (as he had done!) and achieve Nirvana.

What are the Four Noble Truths?

Well, in layman's terms, they are the following:

First Noble Truth: Life is suffering (meaning anything from physical pain to emptiness and mild dissatisfaction; even good things cause our hearts to suffer because we know they will end someday).

Second Noble Truth: The cause of all this suffering is our own egotistical desire for money, possessions, peace, love, life, health, happiness, consistency, comfort—you name it. (In other words: If you didn't want anything, we wouldn't suffer.)

Third Noble Truth: The end of human suffering can be brought about by extinguishing all desire. (Attaining this is called Nirvana.)

Fourth Noble Truth: The Eightfold Path is the way to Nirvana.

Which leads us to our next question: *What is the Eightfold Path*? It's basically a list of lessons for how to live in a way that maximizes the good, minimizes the bad, and eliminates desire.

The path is:

1. **Right Understanding:** Understand things as they are really are (i.e., the Four Noble Truths).
2. **Right Thought:** Act from a place of loving kindness and compassion; practice letting go of your desire for material things; do no harm.
3. **Right Speech:** Be courteous; think before speaking; no lies, back-biting, slandering.
4. **Right Action:** Behave in a peaceful, honorable way; don't steal or destroy life.
5. **Right Livelihood:** Make a living in an industry that does not bring harm to others.
6. **Right Effort:** Extinguish unwholesome qualities (such as greed, anger, and ignorance) while cultivating wholesome ones (such as generosity, loving kindness, and wisdom).
7. **Right Mindfulness:** Be aware and attentive of your body, thoughts and perceptions; note how thoughts appear and disappear within you and how deep breathing can make you more in tune with yourself.
8. **Right Concentration:** Train your mind to meditate in such a way that all judgment of others and ourselves, as well as all desire, goes away, and only pure equanimity is left.

Associated Literary Passages: The Buddha-Carita of Asvaghosa, The Dhammapada, *The Gospel of Buddha* by Paul Carus, and *The Life of Buddha* by Andre Ferdinand Herold, among others

The Food and Fun: Buddhists partake in any number of Asian dishes on Vesak, but consume no meat—a symbol of their compassion for all living things. They also visit monasteries, give to charity, hang lanterns, decorate with flowers, and listen to lessons offered by monks. Often, they'll have parades of musicians, dancers, floats, and dragons. A baby Buddha statue is common, and celebrants often pour water over the statue to symbolize, among other things, a pure and new beginning. Most importantly, Buddhists reaffirm their devotion to the Buddha's precepts and teachings.

Conveying meaning to kids: It's never too early to introduce youngsters to the Buddha and his thoughtful Eightfold Path, and Vesak is a great excuse. You might also consider making paper lanterns or drawing pictures of lotus blossoms. Show your child some pictures of Buddhist monks. Enjoy a vegetarian meal. Make a Buddhist flag, and fly it. If there's one thing I've learned about talking to kids about religion, it's that it really helps to have props; consider picking up a Buddha statue or statuette—something for your child to look at and touch while you talk about Buddhism. Explain a bit about meditation and deep breathing.

CHRISTIANITY

Founded: The first century
Deity: God (The Holy Trinity consists of "God the Father, God the Son, and God the Holy Spirit")
Famous Dogma: Jesus is God's begotten son and died to atone for the sins of all human beings.
Methods of Worship: Prayer, singing, almsgiving, Eucharist/holy communion, and attending church on Sundays (the Christian Sabbath)
Symbol: Cross/Crucifix
Notable Sects: There are more than 30,000 Christian denominations. Three major sects are Catholic, Eastern Orthodox, and Protestant, but the latter includes countless churches. Non-Trinitarian churches include the Church of Jesus Christ of Latter-Day Saints (Mormons).
Number of Followers: 2.1 billion
Sacred Text: The Bible (The Old Testament is everything that is said to have occurred before Jesus' birth, and the New Testament refers to everything after.)
Life-Cycle Celebrations: Baptisms, confirmations, weddings, and

funerals
Traditional Views of Afterlife: Heaven is generally depicted as a perfect place where Jesus resides at the "right hand of the Lord" and where humans can experience life everlasting. Hell is depicted as a place of eternal punishment.
Clothing: Although many Christians wear crosses around their necks, there is no traditional dress for Christian lay people—only clergy. Protestant ministers sometimes wear robes of various colors. Catholic priests wear cassocks and collars. Nuns wear habits. Certain denominations have their own clothing requirements. Mormons wear temple undergarments at all times except for when bathing or swimming. Plain-dress denominations, such as Amish and Mennonites, wear old-timey-looking outfits. (Women wear long dresses, aprons, and bonnets; men wear black trousers, white shirts, and suspenders.) In some plain-dress sects, married men grow out their beards but shave their mustaches, a symbol of their pacifism. (In their early days, European soldiers were known for growing mustaches.)
Major Narrative: The story of Jesus' birth, life, and death—otherwise known as "The Passion"—is the most important story in Christianity. Jesus was from a town called Nazareth but was said to have been born in the city of Bethlehem because his virgin mother, Mary, and her husband, Joseph, had gone there to register for the census. As the story goes: There was no room at the local inn, so Mary wrapped Jesus in cloth and laid him in a manger. Jesus grew up, turned to the ministry, and by the age of thirty-three had amassed a group of followers called the twelve Disciples. At his famous Last Supper in Jerusalem, Jesus instructed his disciples to go out into the world to minister and heal the sick on their own. It was at this point that they became "apostles." But one of the twelve, known as Judas, betrayed Jesus to Roman authorities, who condemned Jesus to die. He was crucified on a cross and his body entombed. On the third day after his crucifixion, Jesus rose from the dead and ascended to heaven. Christians believe Jesus' death brought forgiveness of sins and reconciliation between God and humanity.
Important Holidays: Easter (detailed below), Christmas (detailed below), Pentecost, and Ephiphany.

Christmas
AKA: Christ's Mass
Religion Represented: Christianity
Date: December 25

Celebrates: The birth of Jesus of Nazareth, whom Christians believe is the Messiah, also known as the Christ. The four weeks leading up to December 25 are known as the Advent, a time of spiritual cleansing, renewal, and online shopping.
Star of the Show: Jesus
Back Story: As the story goes, Jesus was born to a virgin mother named Mary, who was miraculously impregnated by the Holy Spirit. In her 6th month of pregnancy, the angel Gabriel appeared and told her Jesus should be "Son of the Highest" and "of his kingdom there shall be no end." Mary went into labor in the city of Bethlehem, where she and her husband, Joseph, had gone to register for the census. There was no room at the local inn, so Mary wrapped the baby in cloth and laid him in a manger. At some later point, a number of magi (astronomers) followed a mysterious star to the house where Jesus was living at that time. They brought the little boy—whom they heralded as the new "King of the Jews"—gifts of gold, frankincense, and myrrh. The story takes a dark twist, however, when King Herod learns that a new king has been born and orders the massacre of all young, male boys in the city Bethlehem—so as to protect his throne.
Associated literary passages: Two passages in the Bible tell the story of Jesus' birth: Matthew 1:18-3:23 and Luke 1:26 and 2:40.
The Food and Fun: Christmas is associated with roast beef, ham, turkey, chestnuts, cranberries, oranges, candy canes, figgy pudding, and something called a fruitcake, which one should never actually consume. For Christians, Christmas is about peace, joy, goodwill, and giving. Lucky for children, the giving part translates into presents. Lots and lots of presents. Usually gifts are placed in stockings (which traditionally hang by the fireplace) and collected under Christmas trees until a grand reveal on Christmas Eve or Christmas morning.
Conveying meaning to kids: Tell the nativity story, followed by *'Twas the Night Before Christmas;* explain the difference. Watch one of the billions of Christmas movies (particularly "Scrooge"—even though your husband might try to tell you that Albert Finney over-acts in the part of Ebenezer Scrooge. He's wrong; be sure to tell him that.) Listen to some Christmas carols—or, better yet, go caroling around your neighborhood.

Participate in a toy drive. Have dinner with your family. And, please, for the sake of your kids, do not underestimate the importance of Christmas crackers. Not only do these British goodies make a fun snap when opened, they contain paper crowns, which, when worn by all your family members at one time, immediately remove any underlying tensions among them. Better still, the little jokes and toys give the kids something to do during what otherwise might be a way-too-formal affair.

Easter
AKA: Resurrection Day
Religion Represented: Christianity
Date: The first Sunday after the full moon following the vernal equinox
Celebrates: The resurrection of Jesus
Star of the Show: Jesus
Back Story: During his lifetime, Jesus of Nazareth never called himself the Messiah or Christ, at least not publicly. But by the time he and his disciples made their way to Jerusalem for Passover in the year 33 CE (or thereabouts), many people believed he was both. As legend has it: Jesus caused a ruckus at the temple in Jerusalem by overturning the tables of some dishonest merchants there—an event that raised the hackles of Roman leaders who already may have felt threatened by Jesus' growing religious (and political) popularity. After hosting his Last Supper (famously depicted by Leonardo da Vinci), Jesus was betrayed by Judas and condemned to die. He was crucified on a wooden cross (the symbol of Christianity) beneath a crown of thorns. On the third day after his crucifixion, according to the Gospels, Jesus rose from the dead and ascended to heaven. Christians believe Jesus' death brought forgiveness of sins and reconciliation between God and humanity. The entire week preceding Easter is called Holy Week and is meant to offer day-by-day reenactments of all that happened to Jesus prior to his death. The week begins with Palm Sunday, which marks the day Jesus arrived in Jerusalem. On Maundy Thursday, Christians commemorate the Last Supper; on Good Friday, they commemorate the decidedly *not* good day of Jesus' crucifixion; and on Holy

Saturday, they commemorate the transition between the crucifixion and resurrection. Holy Week ends with the happiest day of the year: Easter. In a sense, every Sunday of the year is meant to be a mini-celebration of Easter.

Associated Literary Passages: There are many in the New Testament: Matthew 27:50-53; Matthew 28:1-20; Mark 16:1-19; Luke 24:1-53; John 11:25-26; John 20:1-22:25; Romans 1:4-5; Romans 6:8-11; Philippians 3:10-12; and 1 Peter 1:3, among others.

The Food and Fun: Some of what Christians eat on Easter harkens back to the Passover Seder: hard-boiled eggs and lamb, among them. Ham is also an Easter staple, along with chocolate and sweets. In addition to dressing in their "Sunday best" for Easter church services, Christians give to charity, share feasts with family, and give Easter baskets full of chocolates, jellybeans and other goodies to children. Much like the Hindu celebration of Holi, Easter falls at the beginning of spring—so lots of the activities are symbolic of fertility and new life. Eggs, which also are said to represent the empty tomb of Jesus, are central to Easter, with celebrants hard-boiling them, painting them, and hiding them for children. The Easter Bunny, although secular, also has become an Easter mainstay—the equivalent of Santa Claus to Christmas.

Conveying Meaning to Kids: Ironically, secular parents sometimes have an easier time explaining Easter than many Christian parents do. The Passion is just such a damn mystery. Why did Jesus have to suffer? Why didn't God intervene? How, exactly, did Jesus' death bring about forgiveness of human sins? And if Jesus rose from the dead, why can't we? Secular parents are lucky they don't have to try to make sense of all this. Still, it's important to let kids know this story is the single most important one in all of Christianity. If your kid knows this one, the rest is icing. I strongly suggest thumbing through your library's selection of Easter books and staying the heck away from the Berenstain Bears' version. Oh, and *Jesus Christ Super Star* is a great movie for kids, like, ten and up.

ISLAM

Founded: Around 610 CE
Deity: Allah ("The God" in Arabic, pronounced ah-LAW)
Famous Dogma: There is no God but God, and Muhammad is his prophet.
Methods of Worship: Prayer (required five times a day, using prayer mats that face a building called the Kaaba in the middle of Mecca in Saudi Arabia), reciting/singing the Qur'an, almsgiving, and fasting during the month of Ramadan. Formal services occur at mosques every Friday at noon.
Symbol: Star and the crescent
Major Sects: Sunni, Shia, Sufi
Number of Followers: 1.6 billion
Sacred Texts: The Qur'an and the Hadith
Life-Cycle Celebrations: Naming ceremonies, marriages, and pilgrimages to Mecca—which are called Hajj
Traditional Views of Afterlife: Righteous believers—those who pray, donate to charity, read the Qur'an, and believe in one true Allah—are said to go to Jannah, a garden-like place of pleasure. Hell (Jahannam) is depicted as a fiery place where those who do not conform to the teachings of the Qur'an will be banished forever.
Clothing: The Qur'an encourages all Muslim men and women to dress modestly, but some Muslims have interpreted parts of the Qur'an in a way that requires women to wear hijab (pronounced hee-JOB)—clothing that covers the head and/or body. Most American Muslim women wear only head coverings as their hijab, while some Muslim women may be seen in face veils and abayas (uh-BY-yas)—long cloaks worn over their clothing. Only in very strict countries (such as Afghanistan) do women wear hijab in the form of full burkas, which cover their entire bodies, head to toe.
Major Narrative: Born Muhammad ibn Abd Allah ibn Abd al-Muttalib (say that three times fast) in 570 CE in the Arabian city of Mecca, Muhammad was orphaned at age six and placed with family members—first his grandmother and then his uncle. He was a merchant and a shepherd and was known around Mecca as a man of high character. As an adult, Muhammad regularly took a few weeks off to meditate by himself in a nearby cave. During one visit, made when he was forty, Muhammad said he heard a voice speak to him. It was, he later learned, the angel Gabriel (yes, the same Gabriel from Christianity)

acting as a sort of liaison to Allah and delivering messages intended just for him. Allah, Muhammad said, told him that there was only one true Allah, and that Muhammad should call himself a prophet and deliver messages about how to be a good Muslim—that is, to be forgiving, charitable, and empathetic to those less fortunate. Muhammad did as he was told and was said to receive messages from God throughout the next two decades. Those messages eventually were compiled into the Qur'an. Even today, Muhammad is integral to Islam, but not worshipped. Worship is for Allah alone.
Important Holidays: Ramadan (detailed below), Eid ul-Fitr (detailed below), Eid al-Adha, and Mawlid al-Nabi

Ramadan
Pronounced: RAH-muh-don
AKA: Holy Month
Religion Represented: Islam
Date: This month-long holiday takes place during the Islamic calendar's ninth month, which is called—you guessed it—Ramadan.
Celebrates: Charity, self-restraint, and devotion to Allah
Related Holiday: Eid ul-Fitr, which occurs at the end of Ramadan
Star of the Show: Allah
Guest-Starring: The moon
Back Story: Ramadan is considered the holiest month because it was during Ramadan that Allah was said to have first contacted Muhammad. The Qur'an, as a result, makes direct reference to Ramadan and its rituals. Every year, from the first sight of the waxing crescent moon until the last sight of the waning crescent, Muslims throughout the world remember what Allah is said to have told Muhammad about how to be a good Muslim—to be forgiving, charitable and empathetic to those less fortunate. In this way, Muslims are keenly aware of the moon's changes throughout Ramadan. Fasting during Ramadan is one of the Five Pillars of Islam. Although those who are unable to fast—kids, elderly, pregnant women—are specifically excluded from the requirement, the Qur'an makes clear the fasting period (yes, water included) lasts from sunup to sundown every day of the month and that Muslims should also abstain from sex and other worldly temp-

tations as a way to show thanks to Allah and understand what it's like to go without. Today, in Muslim communities throughout the world, food-based businesses close down during the fasting hours to avoid temptation. Muhammad himself celebrated Ramadan until his death.

Associated Literary Passages: The Qur'an Chapter 2: Section 23

The Food and Fun: Not much food, not much fun. During this period, Muslims eat two meals a day during Ramadan—one before dawn and the other after sundown. They pray as much as possible, above and beyond the usual five prayers a day, and they are encouraged to read the Qur'an all the way through. In addition, Ramadan is supposed to be about feeding the poor, forgiving those who have hurt you, and asking forgiveness from those you have hurt. Ramadan is a much-celebrated and revered holiday among Muslims, but—as my husband (who grew up in Saudi Arabia) said—it is also very hard. People who fast get weak and fatigued easily. Keeping your mind on school or work is a challenge, to say the least. The only lifesaver is, at the end of each day, when the sun goes down, Muslims break their fasts with dates and then eat meals that taste, well, flipping amazing after a whole day of nothing. (Dates are the way Muhammad himself broke his fast.) But, truly, the most "fun" part of the holiday occurs at the end of Ramadan—with the holiday of Eid ul-Fitr.

Conveying Meaning to Kids: Ramadan is a great time to do some star-gazing with your kids, to tell them about the cycle of the moon and ponder its remarkable presence in the sky. But more to the point, Ramadan is a great time to give to food pantries and other charities that feed the poor. You might talk a little about the idea of fasting and point out how difficult it can be for people to go that long without food—and how millions of poor people around the globe must fast out of necessity. Also, for the fun of it, check out some Islamic music—*Ramadan Moon* and *A is for Allah* are two great ones by Yusef Islam. In addition to *Ramadan* by Susan L. Douglass, check out *Night of the Moon: A Muslim Holiday Story* by Hena Khan and Julie Paschkis or *Celebrating Ramadan* by Diane Hoyt-Goldsmith.

Eid al-Fitr
Pronounced: EED uhl-FIT-er
AKA: "Festivity for Breaking the Fast"
Religion Represented: Islam
Date: The first day of the Islamic month of Shawwal
Celebrates: The end of Ramadan
Back Story: Eid al-Fitr exists because Ramadan exists. While the Qur'an never mentions Eid ul-Fitr, it was a holiday celebrated by Muhammad and is considered (by most) just as holy. Eid services are always held in huge outdoor venues, which ensure that many people can come together. Muslims are required to bathe (cleanliness is extremely important in Islam, to the point where bathing facilities are often included in mosque design), dress in their finest clothes, wear perfume, and arrive early at the worship service. (Waiting is considered a virtue.) Weather permitting, Muslims walk to the service while reciting the following: "Allahu-Akbar, Allahu-Akbar. La ila-ha ill-lallah. . . . Wa-lilahill hamd." This translates from Arabic as: "Allah is the Greatest, Allah is the Greatest. There is no god but Allah. . . . All praises are for Allah."
Associated Literary Passages: There are none
The Food and Fun: In many ways, Eid ul-Fitr is a lot like Christmas. In addition to attending formal worship services, everyone wears the best clothes they own (and often receive new clothing as gifts). They decorate their homes, cook huge feasts, and exchange presents. Sometimes feasts are laid out on rugs in front of houses, so people can wander from one home to the next, trying out a little of everything. In this way, Eid creates a communal atmosphere, where the fortunate and the unfortunate mix together. Giving to the poor is not only emphasized; it is required. Charity is carried out in numerous ways. Some give their money, others their time. It is customary in many countries, such as Saudi Arabia, to put together baskets of food and leave them on people's doorsteps, or buy gifts for children and then hand them out in the streets.
Conveying Meaning to Kids: I think one of the best things we can do in our own Islamaphobic country is to familiarize our kids with Muslim people—their dress, their beliefs, and their rituals. Play some Yusef Islam music. Have a movie night. Show *Muhammad: The Last Prophet,* an animated film

about Muhammad's life, intended for small children. Or, for slightly older children, there's *Koran by Heart,* a touching HBO documentary that follows three ten-year-old Muslim children.

ENDNOTES

1 "'Nones' on the Rise," Pew Research Religion & Public Life Project. Accessed September 28, 2014, http://www.pewforum.org/2012/10/09/nones-on-the-rise/.

2 "Pope Francis Says Atheists Who Do Good Are Redeemed, Not Just Catholics," *Huffington Post*, May 22, 2013.

3 David Niose, *Nonbeliever Nation: The Rise of Secular Americans* (New York: Palgrave MacMillan, 2012), 11.

4 "'Nones' on the Rise," Pew Research Religion & Public Life Project. Accessed September 28, 2014, http://www.pewforum.org/2012/10/09/nones-on-the-rise/.

5 "Faith on the Hill" Pew Research Centers Religion & Public Life Project, January 2, 2013.

6 2001 ARIS Report, American Religious Identification Surveys. Accessed October 7, 2014, http://commons.trincoll.edu/aris/publications/2001-2/aris-2001-report/.

7 Niose, *Non-believer Nation*.

8 "'Nones' on the Rise," Pew Research Religion & Public Life Project. Accessed September 28, 2014, http://www.pewforum.org/2012/10/09/nones-on-the-rise/.

9 "Atheists, Muslims See Most Bias as Presidential Candidates," GALLUP. June 21, 2012. Accessed October 7, 2014, http://www.gallup.com/poll/155285/Atheists-Muslims-Bias-Presidential-Candidates.aspx.

10 Christel J. Manning, "Unaffiliated Parents and the Religious Training of Their Children," *Sociology of Religion*. Accessed October 7, 2014, http://socrel.oxfordjournals.org/content/early/2013/01/16/socrel.srs072.

11 Phil Zuckerman, "Atheism, Secularity, and Well-Being: How the Findings of Social Science Counter Negative Stereotypes and Assumptions," *Sociology Compass*. Accessed October 7, 2014, https://www.pitzer.edu/academics/faculty/zuckerman/Zuckerman_on_Atheism.pdf.

12 KJ Dell'Antonia, "The Danger of Not Talking to Your Children About Race," *Motherlode* (blog), *New York Times*, April 14, 2012, http://parenting.blogs.nytimes.com/?s=danger+of+not+talking+to+children+about+race.

13 Todd Parr, *The Okay Book* (Sydney: ABC Books for the Australian Broadcasting, 2008).

14 "Dr. Robert J. Lifton's Eight Criteria for Thought Reform," International Cultic Studies Association. Accessed November 14, 2014, www.csj.org/infoserv_articles/lifton_robert_thoughtreform_abs.htm.

15 Brian Flood, "Study finds moral equality between religious, nonreligious," UIC News Center. September 11, 2014. Accessed October 8, 2014, news.uic.edu/study-finds-moral-equality-between-religious-nonreligious.

16 D'Arcy Lyness, "Teaching Your Child Tolerance," *KidsHealth*. March 1, 2014. Accessed October 8, 2014, kidshealth.org/parent/positive/talk/tolerance.html#.

17 Richard Wade, "Ask Richard: Teaching My Kids Religious Tolerance and Science at the Same Time," *Friendly Atheist* (blog). October 4, 2010. Accessed November 18, 2014, www.patheos.com/blogs/friendlyatheist/2010/10/04/ask-richard-teaching-my-kids-religious-tolerance-and-science-at-the-same-time.

18 Gordon W. Allport, *The Nature of Prejudice* (Cambridge, Mass.: Addison-Wesley, 1954). Accessed November 18, 2014, http://faculty.washington.edu/caporaso/courses/203/readings/allport_Nature_of_Prejudice.pdf.

19 Karyn Henley and Dennas Davis, *The Beginner's Bible: Timeless Children's Stories* (Sisters, Ore.: Questar, 1989).

20 Stephen R. Prothero, *Religious Literacy: What Every American Needs to Know—And Doesn't* (San Francisco: Harper San Francisco, 2007), 136.

21 Hailey Woldt, "A New Model Of Teaching Religious Tolerance," *The Huffington Post*. October 17, 2012. Accessed October 8, 2014, http://www.huffingtonpost.com/hailey-woldt/teaching-religious-tolerance-is-scary_b_1962185.html.

22 Alain de Botton, *Religion for Atheists: A Non-believer's Guide to the Uses of Religion* (New York: Pantheon Books, 2013).

23 Richard Wade, "Ask Richard: My Zealous Catholic Parents Are Indoctrinating My Kids," *Friendly Atheist*, December 27, 2010. Accessed November 18, 2014, www,patheos.com/blogs/friendlyatheist/2010/12/27/ask-richard-my-catholic-parents-are-indoctrinating-my-kids/.

24 Earl A. Grollman, *Talking About Death: A Dialogue Between Parent and Child* (Boston: Beacon Press, 1990).

25 George A. Bonanno, *The Other Side of Sadness: What the New Science of Bereavement Tells Us About Life After Loss* (New York: Basic Books, 2009), 42.

ABOUT THE AUTHOR

Wendy Thomas Russell is an award-winning journalist, author and secular-parenting blogger. A native Midwesterner and former newspaper reporter, Russell and her work have been featured in numerous publications, both print and online. She lives in Long Beach, California, with her husband and daughter and can be found, virtually speaking, at www.wendythomasrussell.com or on Twitter @WendyRussell.

BROWN
PAPER
PRESS

Brown Paper Press engages readers on topics of contemporary culture through quality writing and thoughtful design. Unbound by genre, our press delivers socially relevant works that advise, guide, inspire, and amuse. We champion authors with new perspectives, strong voices, and original ideas that just might change the world.

For more information, please visit us at www.brownpaperpress.com.

CPSIA information can be obtained at www.ICGtesting.com
Printed in the USA
LVOW08s2131161215

466813LV00006B/448/P